The Sacraments in Methodism

Robert W. Goodloe

THE METHODIST PUBLISHING HOUSE

NASHVILLE	CINCINNATI	CHICAGO	NEW YORK
DALLAS	RICHMOND	BALTIMORE	KANSAS CITY
DETROIT	PITTSBURGH	PORTLAND	SAN FRANCISCO

1953

THE SACRAMENTS IN METHODISM

Copyright MCMLIII by Pierce & Washabaugh

Library of Congress Catalog Card Number: 52-13755

SET UP, PRINTED, AND BOUND BY THE
PARTHENON PRESS, AT NASHVILLE,
TENNESSEE, UNITED STATES OF AMERICA

The Sacraments in Methodism

Contents

Foreword

The Sacraments in Methodism is written in recognition of a growing interest in ceremonial worship and in encouragement of that form of worship. Although it came into existence as a denomination seventeen hundred years after the rise of Christianity, Methodism considers itself a legitimate branch of the historic Church, having been called into existence by the same Holy Spirit which was promised by the Lord "to guide you into all truth."

In every age and among all worshiping bodies, religious ceremonies grow out of and express the basic theology of the people. To this end, and to state that Methodists follow the emphasis of Protestantism upon justification by faith, the second chapter discusses the topic, "By Grace Are Ye Saved Through Faith." This section is followed by an explanation of the general Methodist view of religious ceremonies as "Means of Grace."

Methodists do not consider ordination a sacrament. In that teaching they follow the Church of England, out of which body the church sprang, seeing that for some seven hundred years Anglicanism has declared its faith in baptism and the Lord's Supper, and has rejected the other five sacraments of historic Catholic practice. But since by ordination The Methodist Church sets apart ministers to their tasks, it seems well that this custom be explained here.

ROBERT W. GOODLOE

7

1.

The Church, Which
Is His Body

THE FIRST element in the Church is God, his purpose and work as revealed in Christ Jesus; and the second necessary factor is a body of believers in God, organized to carry on his work and to worship him. As Dr. Clarence Tucker Craig words it: "Wherever the saving grace of God in Christ is manifest, there is the Church." The Church is the sphere of his salvation; it is composed of those to whom he has brought redemption. Then referring to the Ephesian description of the Church, Dr. Craig continues: "Those who call upon the name of the Lord in faith, who are baptized in his name, have received the Spirit which he gives, and look forward to the consummation of his kingdom—these belong to his body and are the people whom God has called for himself." And bringing this New Testament principle down to our times, the same writer reasons: "Though they may be organized in different ways for worship and for the expression of their community life, they all belong to the one Church of God, for they all share in his salvation."

"CHURCH" IN THE NEW TESTAMENT

The word "Church" is found more than one hundred times in the New Testament. "In seventy-nine times it is used of

9

the local church, either in the singular or plural; in twenty-seven times it is used of the church universal." Paul applied the word both to local congregations and to the universal body. He speaks frequently of the "churches" of a group (Gentiles) or of an area (Galatia, Macedonia, Judaea). "Especially interesting is his reference to some particular group of disciples meeting in a given house as a Church ('the Church that is in their house')."

It is not only that the one spiritual body of Christ takes visible and empirical form in local congregations of believers, but these are all joined in vital union to Christ. Christ dwells in them and any one of these would be the Church of Christ if all others should disappear. Indeed, each one of them is the Church of Christ in that particular place.[1]

THE CHURCH BOTH HUMAN AND DIVINE

As the Creed of Chalcedon declared that in Jesus there are "two natures in one Person," so in the Church there are two natures in one body. The real confusion arises when one fails to keep clear the relation between the kingdom of God on the one hand and the Church here on earth on the other hand. "Just as the Holy Spirit of God is itself perfect and yet operative in a sinful world, so the Church, . . . insofar as it represents the efforts of men, is touched with imperfection." The Church is divine, then, in the sense that it belongs to God, and through it he is doing his work in the world. The Church is human in the sense that it is the fellowship of those who belong to Christ and are being made over in holiness of character and life. This element of imperfection, the human element, is clear in the writings of Paul. Hardly has he greeted "them that are sanctified" before he takes up

[1] Harris F. Rall, *According to Paul*, pp. 162-63.

the matter of their endless disputes. He says of them, "Ye are washed, . . . ye are sanctified;" yet he calls them carnal, and censures the jealousy and strife which are in their midst. The human aspect—as well as the divine—is very real, for in it God and man come together for the saving of men.

THE CHURCH A CONTINUING AGENCY

"As my Father hath sent me, even so send I you." "Go ye into all the world, and preach the gospel to every creature. He that believeth and is baptized shall be saved; but he that believeth not shall be damned." Such is the continuation of that process which began with the Word in the world, was carried forward with the Word in Israel, and reached its perfect manifestation in Jesus Christ. It is the "little flock," the "leaven" which leavens the world, and the "salt of the earth" which preserves the world. "In reality, the Church is Christ manifest in the flesh, as Jesus of Nazareth was God manifest in the flesh."

From the third century has come the motto: "He who does not have the Church for his mother cannot have God for his Father." The same confident idea is worded in the Westminster Confession: "The Church is the house and family of God, outside of which there is no ordinary means of salvation." The ritual for reception of members into The Methodist Church enlarges upon this conception:

The Church is of God, and will be preserved to the end of time, for the promotion of his worship and the due administration of his word and ordinances, the maintenance of Christian fellowship and discipline, the edification of believers, and the conversion of the world. All, of every age and station, stand in need of the means of grace which it alone supplies.

11

The Church is what it is because Jesus was what he was. It matters little where one begins his study of the Church, for eventually he will come to the starting point in history— Jesus Christ. One may begin with asking about the congregation in which he worships Sunday after Sunday, or about one across the street which follows very different creeds and customs. In either case those gathered there are a part of that line of witnesses to the truth of what happened during a certain thirty-year period long ago. Should one go to the other side of the globe, to a mission station in India, or to a hospital in the Congo, he would find that these institutions were founded there by men who themselves had heard a message which had come to them through the centuries of Christian history. If one's curiosity was not yet satisfied, he could retrace the steps of those pioneers of the gospel until he arrived in an upper room in Palestine. On that last evening with his followers in the flesh the Master was saying, "Do this in memory of me;" and the same Lord a few days later proclaimed to the same group, as he ascended out of their sight, "Go ye into all the world, and preach the gospel." Today, more than nineteen centuries later, these commands are still being obeyed by increased thousands in every land in the world. "The Church can be understood only as the outcome of those very events which the New Testament records and which the Church still exists to proclaim."

THE CHRISTIAN CHURCH A FULFILLMENT OF GOD'S PURPOSE

The Old Testament tells the story of how God made himself known through the course of Hebrew history. During a famine the sons of Jacob had gone down into Egypt to secure food, and there they had been enslaved. Moses heard the Spirit's call before the burning bush and led the children of Israel safely away from the pursuing army of Pharaoh and through the dangers of the Red Sea. In the wilderness of Sinai the people worshiped, Moses received the Ten Commandments from on high, and Jehovah entered into a covenant with Israel. From that day the people of Israel were to be his people, and he was to be their God. Moving in that faith victory came to their arms as they crossed into the land of promise. But once they had settled in Canaan, the high ideals of the desert days grew dim; and, as Amos and his successors declared, the inevitable consequence of Israel's infidelity was the long night of foreign invasion and ultimate conquest by their enemies. Through the return from exile and in the opportunity to rebuild the despoiled Temple on Mount Zion, Jehovah once again showed his mercy and offered his people a second chance. What tragedy that they failed again—failed in their divine vocation of being "a light to the Gentiles," of bringing the knowledge of God and his purposes to all the nations of earth!

THE NEW COVENANT A FULFILLMENT OF THE OLD COVENANT

This new covenant, represented by Jesus and his Church, was foreseen by Jeremiah: "Behold, the days come, saith the Lord, that I will make a new covenant with the house of Israel. . . . I will put my law in their inward parts, and write it in their hearts; and will be their God, and they shall be my people." Concerning this new covenant the writer of the First Epistle of Peter declares: "Ye are an elect race, a royal priesthood, a holy nation, a people for God's own possession, that ye may show forth the excellencies of him who called you out of darkness into his marvellous light:

13

who in time past were no people, but now are the people of God." The writer here is speaking to Christians in a new Israel, not drawn from only one nation but from many races and kindreds and tribes. And he regards them as the new "royal priesthood" which shall fulfill the vocation which was given to the old Israel, but which that people failed to accomplish.

In this new covenant Jesus was fulfilling the old covenant. His crowning work on earth was the founding of the Church, through which was to be continued the ministry he had begun in Galilee and Jerusalem. Just when and where did this ministry of Christ really begin? That is, how was the Christian Church related to Jehovah and to the earlier Jewish Church?

Through Moses, Amos, and the Prophet of the Exile, God was preparing the way for the Incarnation. . . . "God, who at sundry times and in divers manners spake in time past unto the fathers by the prophets, hath in these last days spoken unto us by his Son." So said the early Christians, when they endeavored to trace to its source the river of grace which sprang forth from the Cross; and so, too, say we.[2]

The Fourth Gospel answers best of all the question of when the work of Jesus began. "In the beginning," it says, "was the Word, and the Word was with God, and the Word was God. . . . And the Word was made flesh, and dwelt among us." The Christian Church has as its function the continuation of the eternal work of the Almighty, and it has as its authority the God who spoke first through patriarch and prophet, then through his Son, and since that

[2] Walter M. Horton, *Realistic Theology*, pp. 140-41.

14

time through the Comforter, whom Jesus said he would send to guide men into all truth.

THE CHRISTIAN CHURCH SET APART

Rather than being antagonistic to the Old Testament church and its ideals, the early Christians thought of themselves as perpetuating all that had been good in that Jewish tradition and fellowship. Once Israel had been the nation. When the nation proved false to God, then Israel meant the faithful remnant—the Jewish Church. But the Jewish Church had refused the Messiah, and now the disciples held themselves to be the true Israel.

Jesus and the Twelve had long worshiped in the synagogue, thinking of themselves as the true Israel—the continuation of the real Old Testament church. It is true that the Master voiced criticism of the "church" in his day; but such protests were never against the temple, only against the abuses connected with it. The earliest recorded sermon of Jesus is said to have been delivered as a part of the normal Sabbath worship in the synagogue of his home town. The New Testament gives account of numerous occasions on which he delivered some teaching or worked some miracle in the synagogue. Luke records that the disciples were "continually in the temple, praising and blessing God."

But the time came when Christians were denied fellowship in the synagogue, and so separate meetings were held. These seem to have been the earliest distinctively "Christian" assemblies. How like the experience of Charles Wesley, who, having taken with him into the Church of England worship service half a dozen of his "Methodists," and having been driven from the Lord's table there, withdrew and for the

15

first time administered the sacred elements to a group of Methodists alone, in an unconsecrated building!

The New Testament account of Paul's missionary travels shows that he sought to share in the services of the synagogues at Salamis, Antioch, Iconium, Philippi, Thessalonica, Berea, Athens, Corinth, and Ephesus. As opposition increased and the apostles or their colleagues were excluded from the regular Jewish services, a decision had to be made. The Acts of the Apostles preserves what seems to be a clear example of this "migration" of Christians from Jews. Paul came to Corinth, and the Roman Jew Aquila and Priscilla, his wife, opened their home; in similar manner arose many a "church in thy house." Thus the separation of Christianity from Judaism was on its way.

As the doors of the churches in England were closed to Wesley, and Asbury and Lee and McKendree in America were refused the privilege of preaching in the regular church buildings in the communities where they traveled, both in England and in America these early Methodists turned to courthouses and store buildings and street corners where they might proclaim the word of God.

THE ROMAN CATHOLIC CONCEPTION OF THE CHURCH

By the time the last of the apostles had finished his work the Christian Church had become consciously separate from the Jewish Church. Paul had organized Christian groups from Jerusalem to Rome. The rebellion of the Jews against the empire, around A.D. 70, brought destruction to their capital city and the end of Israel as an independent nation. With Jewish worship prohibited in Palestine and with the scattering of Jews and Christians throughout the empire, the Christian Church became increasingly Gentile both in membership and in ministry. This shift in geography and constituency brought significant changes in the Christian Church. Within one hundred years after the death of the last apostle the teaching of Jesus and the customs of the early Christian bodies were no longer being interpreted by Jews but by Gentiles.

The Scriptures speak of Jesus as having come in the "fulness of the time"; that is, the prophetic conception of God as the Father of all men and races, not simply of the Jews, had become sufficiently recognized as to make it possible for Jesus to proclaim his message. And yet how slowly Jesus promulgated this idea. How slowly even his own disciples grasped the universal meaning of God; and so opposed were "orthodox" Jews that they crucified the Lord. But the prophetic understanding of God as manifested in Jesus—that Jew and Gentile are one in his sight—became the distinctive Christian message. Every man who desires to do so may have the benefits of God's blessing.

Up until that time—in state and in church—each race had thought of itself as separate from the others and of other people as its enemies. The bringing together of the many races and territories around the Mediterranean into one state, the Roman Empire, was but the application of this universal conception. All the peoples of the old world which hitherto had lived and labored apart—all their gains and achievements, their ancient traditions and legends, their gods and rites and worship, all existing elements of culture and forces of civilization—were now comprised in one empire. The thought of a religion not national but for all races could not have been appreciated by the people of an earlier age. Now that the old nationalities had been demolished, the thought of a kingdom of God embracing all nations could strike root. It was

17

into this "fulness of time" that Paul came to work as the "Apostle to the Gentiles," planting the Church in Asia Minor and even in Rome.

Jesus had "broken down the middle wall of partition" between Jew and Gentile, bringing in those interpretations of religion which made the Christian Church a body different from that of the Jews. Two or three centuries later when Christians—almost exclusively Gentiles—set down their understandings of the teachings of Jesus and Christian institutions, what a different picture was presented. By A.D. 400 Baptism was already assuming the idea of regeneration, the elements of the Lord's Supper were being spoken of as the flesh and blood of the crucified Lord, and a kind of motto had been established: "He who does not have the Church for his mother cannot have God for his Father." The early Christian Church had become the Catholic Church. This significant change had been made without council or convention as gradually as the Christian Church had become separate from the Jewish Church or The Methodist Church would become distinct from the Church of England.

And it must never be forgotten that in the Catholic Church the early Christian people did not cease to be legitimate successors of the primitive age. Dr. Schaff explains: "While far inferior in originality, purity, energy, and freshness," this Church of the second and third centuries "is distinguished for conscientious fidelity in preserving and propagating the sacred writings and traditions of the apostles, and for untiring zeal in imitating their holy lives amidst the greatest difficulties and dangers, when the religion of Christ was prohibited by law and the profession of it punished as a political crime." The author continues in expression of what strengthens and cheers our faith:

18

No merely human religion could have stood such an ordeal of fire for three hundred years. The final victory of Christianity over Judaism and heathenism, and the mightiest empire of the ancient world . . . is one of the sublimest spectacles in history, and one of the strongest evidences of the divinity and indestructible life of our religion.[3]

EACH DENOMINATION A MEMBER OF THE CHURCH

The fullness of life and truth, as Christ has revealed it, is too vast to be understood in exactly the same way by all persons. The first generation of believers in Jesus Christ was not the last to contrast the emphasis of a Peter with the interpretation of a Paul. There will almost certainly always be persons who feel the need of a Church which possesses authority. They think of it "as a supernatural institution, divinely inaugurated at a specific moment in history, miraculously endowed from above with efficacious sacraments and with a God-given ordination for effective ministry."[4]

This way of thinking has come to them out of their own individual temperaments, and from the general society in which they have been born and reared; it has been thus through the centuries, wherever any measure of freedom has been allowed the individual, and probably will be so to the end.

But just as certainly there are persons who, like Dr. Rufus Jones, "feel assured in their own soul's experience that there is a divine light planted in man's inmost being which makes it possible for persons like us to have direct intimate communion and fellowship with God here and now."[5] This

[3] Philip Schaff, *History of the Christian Church*, II, 7-8.
[4] Rufus M. Jones, *A Preface to Christian Faith in a New Age*, p. 154. Used by permission.
[5] *Ibid.*, p. 155.

proportion of the total church membership has increased as the democratic practices of life have spread. So that if peace and freedom come and abide, the demand for High-Church forms of worship will decrease as time goes on; and as the democratic way of life and thought prevails, then forms of worship which give the individual member a larger participation in group activity and a more direct fellowship with God will probably mark the dominant type of church and officer and sacrament.

Persons who live and work in the joy of this fellowship desire no other kind of authority than that which is within.

They do not feel like aliens and foreigners here in the world of time, who need special ambassadors commissioned to speak for a distant Sovereign. Their hearts burn with the consciousness of a living Presence here and now. They live their lives and do their work with a sense of unsundered correspondence with their Great Companion. For them a Church is a Fellowship of those who believe in, live by, and share in this presence of God.[6]

This Quaker conception of closeness to God, this idea of fellowship, was prominent among those who lived and labored with Jesus here on the earth; it was the distinctive feature of the New Testament Church. That is the reason we have so little of definite "legislation" in the accounts of the Church in that period. As the Church passed out of that New Testament sharing into the more legalistic way of life in the wide Roman Empire, it took on the characteristics of the later Catholic Church. In that church one finds very specific legislation for almost every phase of life—officers must be ordained and authorized in a specific manner; the sacraments follow very rigid and definite rules; and the experience of "fellowship"

[6] *Ibid.*, p. 153.

one with another, and of direct relation to God, almost ceases to be.

But since there is today—and has been in a marked form since the time of Martin Luther—a people with a very different basic experience in their total life, then the Church which serves them will have to modify the agencies and conceptions which were normal to the people of the Roman Empire. It is not that the Catholic way of worship is wrong nor that the way of life distinctive of Protestantism is mistaken; it is rather that these different forms correspond to the needs of different individuals, and so these newer types of churches must be allowed freedom equal to that of the older ones. Then all may be best served and given that full realization of God which is normal to each.

The atmosphere of rivalry, the insistence upon exclusive possession of truth, the hardness of heart which goes with that state of mind—all defeat the very aim and function of a Church of Christ.

There can be no true and legitimate place for denominational Church families unless they can be genuine organic spiritual members of one unified Body of Christ builded together for a habitation of God in the Spirit. Such a consummation seems no doubt like a dream, a far-off event that could come only by miracle. But something very much like miracles have had a way of happening in the course of Christian history. All that would be needed to ensure this consummation would be the actual answer to the prayer of benediction which all churches pray each week: "May the grace of the Lord Jesus Christ and the love of God and the fellowship of the holy spirit be with you and in you all." [7]

[7] *Ibid.*, p. 160.

THE RELATION OF METHODISM TO THE CHURCH

"Methodism is not of men but of God," declared Dr. Hugh Price Hughes in the presidential address to the Wesleyan Conference in 1898. Never overlooking the necessity of human agency—as inferred in the command of the Master, "Go ye into all the world, and preach the gospel"—Dr. Hughes yet maintained that proper balance between the human and the divine as he explained: "I entirely agree . . . that the real founder of Methodism was not John Wesley, but Jesus Christ." From the time of Wesley, Methodists have shared that conviction; and it has molded their beliefs as to the nature of the Church, its ministry, and its sacraments. Following the lead of Methodism's greatest systematic theologian, William Burt Pope, that the Holy Spirit, in all ages and among all groups, directs in founding and governing the Church, Dr. Newton Flew voices his conviction: "The Spirit of God called Methodism into being through the preaching of the Word, just as the Spirit of God has been manifest in the raising up of the other great confessional Churches of Christendom." Dr. H. B. Workman, in the generation just closed, reasoned "that in the affairs of the Church human nature exists . . . we do not deny. But, in considering the final design, it is the Potter that counts even more than the clay; the wheel and the Hand that turns it are fashioning an ordered result." "Every communion of thinkers, every phase of faith, has its place in and its relation to the great whole, and plays some part . . . in the progress and development of the one Holy Catholic Church."

Methodists believe, as did the earliest Fathers, that "where Jesus Christ is, there is His Church." For us, as for Ignatius,

22

"Our charter is Jesus Christ; our infallible charter is his Cross, and his death, and his resurrection, and faith through him." Methodism continues in its *Discipline* Wesley's "General Rules of the United Societies." The description of a society given there is our most satisfactory definition of a church: "A company of men having the form and seeking the power of godliness, united in order to pray together, to receive the word of exhortation, and to watch over one another in love, that they may help each other to work out their salvation."

2.

By Grace Are Ye Saved
Through Faith

IN THE chapter following that in which he speaks of "the church, which is his body," the author of the Epistle to the Ephesians declares, "For by grace are ye saved through faith." In effect the writer is saying, "The first step in man's salvation must be taken by someone outside himself!" That is one with the teaching of the whole Bible. God is our creator; he provides a normal environment for our growth. Even if we sin, he stands ready to redeem and start us on our way again.

This help from outside oneself, this "grace," is necessary because sin weakens a man's ability to think and act in the realm of moral behavior; his moral perception becomes duller and his power of resistance to evil weaker. Both scripture and experience show that the individual cannot swerve from the law that governs the healthy religious development of human nature without dwarfing his own soul and injuring humanity in this life. It is simply the application of the law that as a man soweth, so also shall he reap.

Another consequence of sin is that it leads to distrust in and fear of God. It tends to separate the sinner from God. Genesis gives us that picture in the very beginning of the race. God said to Adam and Eve, You may eat of the fruit of all the trees of the garden except the tree of the knowledge

of good and evil; do not eat of that fruit, for if you do it
will bring death upon you. Then, as we would say in our
family relations, the Father went away for the day. During
the day the children disobeyed. They ate of that forbidden
fruit, and with what consequence! When the Father re-
turned home, and they heard him walking in the garden in
the evening, Adam and Eve were afraid. Reminded now of
the broken command, they were not only ashamed but also
fearful lest the Lord punish them. They looked at the Lord
"through the veil of their sins." They thought of him as
angry with them. God had done no wrong, but his children
had! And the children attributed to God the same change
of attitude that came to them as a result of their wrongdoing.

That experience of our first parents is exactly our thought
today. When we have injured a person, committed some
wrong against him, a barrier arises between his life and ours.
If, while we are walking down the street, we see him coming in our direction, we cross to the other side; we do not
want to meet him. In reality the one against whom we have
acted may not be angry with us; his thought instead may be
one of disappointment, of sorrow; and he may be anxious
to help restore us to good relations with himself. But not
waiting to learn of his attitude toward us in our meanness,
we attribute to him what we would call the normal consequence of our action: that he would want to hurt us! "We
transfer our changed attitude to him. . . . We interpret all
his actions through the shadow which our deed has created.
Our sense of wrongdoing makes us afraid of the person
wronged." [1]

[1] Rufus M. Jones, *The Double Search*, pp. 63-64. Used by permission of publisher, John C. Winston Co.

And what is more damaging to the one who has sinned is that his sin becomes a very part of him. If the consequences of wrongdoing were simply like a load, then it might be lifted from our shoulders either by ourselves or by another; if it were a debt, then it might be paid, and the debtor would be the same as he was before that obligation had been incurred. But such is not the nature of sin. Sin becomes a part of the man who has sinned, and so on the next day after the commission of a sin the man is not what he was the day before it was perpetrated. He is what he was, minus that normal manhood which was taken away by his sin! Evil and impurity have entered his very self, and every understanding of life and experience is modified by the weakened conscience which is the result of the wrong he has committed. His lament is Paul's "O wretched man that I am"—he is wretched, for guilt is now an integral part of himself.

In such a case forgiveness is not enough. We need more than assurance that the past is forgiven and will not count against us on the books. Cancellation would be sufficient if salvation were only a matter of bookkeeping. "We want blackness replaced by whiteness, we want weakness replaced by power, we want to experience a new set of our innermost nature which will make us more than conquerors." [2]

WHAT THE SINNER CANNOT DO FOR HIMSELF

This fact, that the action becomes a part of the actor, is after all the gravest consequence of sin. Paul calls it "the law of sin." Here is a man who is immoral and unholy. By what possible means can he actually become moral and

[2] *Ibid.,* p. 62.

26

holy? The earnest hope of all those about him is that he may cease to be what he is, that he may become that which now he is not. But how can such a change be made? "Instinctively you rather ask, who is there about him? has he a mother? a sister? a high-principled companion? a really good friend? If he has, *there*, you say at once, is the point of hope." All such considerations find their answer ultimately in the great declaration of John's Gospel: "God so loved the world." It is impossible to emphasize too much the fact that "in this whole field of experience the first step is, and remains with God. . . . When our eyes open spiritually, the first object on which they light . . . is a gracious God, who is calling sinners unto himself."

That was the work and experience of Jesus Christ himself while on earth and the task of "the church, which is his body" in the generations following the days of our Lord. Wherever Jesus went, in Judaea or in Galilee, he awakened in men a consciousness of sin and a longing after a better life. However hurtful it may be, sin does not so completely take away from men their ability to exercise choice in the moral realm as to allow them to do what is wrong without a sense of regret. But the actions of many individuals confirm the view that sinful men, left to themselves, do not "turn to God" with sufficient vigor as to become "new creatures."

It is at this point that we come upon the necessity of the work of Jesus Christ, of the grace of God! In the presence of Jesus we know at once that we ought to be like him but that we are not. By simply *declaring* men sinners Jesus does not condemn humankind; rather, by setting before them the reality of his own purity he enables men to make a

27

true estimate of themselves and to turn about in their course.

GOD TAKES THIS FIRST STEP

The figure used in the Old Testament to represent the taking away of sin is the scapegoat. That animal is pictured as having man's sin loaded on his back and then being driven away. The need for such a solution is real, for man cannot undo his own past. It is true also that someone other than the sinner must do what the sinner cannot do; and so in this theological solution the scapegoat is given as the agent for "taking away the sins of the world." How striking and representative it is; but of course we readers of today know, as did the Old Testament writers, that the scapegoat is simply a figure. We realize that every sin bears its hurtful consequence and that guilt can be taken away only as the sinner and he who helps the sinner pay a terrible price. The real question becomes, "How are ignorant, weak, willful, sinful men to be recovered from unrighteousness and developed into the life of God?" This is where the work of Christ comes in as a necessary part of the redeeming action of grace. As the New Testament declares it: "God was in Christ, reconciling the world unto himself."

GOD'S LOVE HELPS MEN BECOME GOOD

No parent looks forward to or plans the degradation of his child. But in spite of all that a father may do, the child sometimes brings degradation upon himself. The father is not guilty; his honor is stainless, but not so the child's. What can the father do, what *must* the father do, if he really is a father? Should he shut himself up within his innocence and nurture his wound until it festers? Only by taking the shame of his child upon himself is he able to maintain his own good character and make that effort essential to the possible restoration of his child. He who was "wounded for our transgressions" took this step. In being "bruised for our iniquities" he was helping to lead men back into a life of holiness.

"THE GRACE OF GOD" THE FIRST STEP

God's laws are for the purpose not of limiting men but of guiding men in the ideals of life. In the same sense in which it may be said that man is the aim and end of creation, so also it may be declared that the purpose of God's laws is the development and perfection of his creatures. The state enacts laws for the protection and welfare of its citizens. Parents lay down regulations for the family in the hope that profit may come thereby for all. In a sense, then, laws express the ideal for man and are intended to aid in his achievement.

Furthermore, the same God who made laws for the guidance of his children stands ready to help carry out those laws to the end for which they were created. This idea is expressed by Paul when he writes, "By the grace of God I am what I am." The desire to help is the normal relation of a father to his child, be the parent human or divine. We see the same reality in nature, for there life has a curative as well as a creative aspect; it expresses itself in the healing of injuries as well as in normal growth. "That life at the Divine level should manifest itself . . . in healing as well as in creating, is only what we should expect."

God is not interested in punishing men, but he does want to help them to achieve his likeness in their lives. In a note to his German translator Ibsen recognized this truth when he wrote, "In every new poem or play I have aimed at my

29

own spiritual emancipation and purification—for a man shares the responsibility and the guilt of the society to which he belongs." [3] Jesus realized this responsibility in his relationship to the children of men, and he met the responsibility by setting himself resolutely to save them from their sins. He considered that the human brotherhood in its sinfulness required nothing less of him.

Without any disturbing consciousness of having personally added to the world's evil, with no plea for pardon for his own sins on his lips but only for those of others, his conscience was burdened with the injustice and disloyalties, the brutalities and failures, of the family of God, in which he was a Son, and he bore his brother's sins on his spirit, and gave himself to the utmost to end them.[4]

God not only desires sonship in us, but he feels the loss and wrong of our sins. "Absalom has broken his father's heart; and we are Absalom. The grand old king goes up over Olivet weeping, with his head covered and his feet bare; and that king is God. . . . This agony of God over human sin is the Lamb slain from the foundation of the world." [5] It is the grace involved in "God so loved the world."

The suffering of Jesus on the cross was an expression of this attitude of God; through Jesus' life and teaching and death we have revealed to us the "lovingkindness" of God toward all his children. If we are loyal, then this grace "will guide you into all truth." If we are disobedient, then that willingness of God to suffer in order to help draw us back becomes "the conviction of the Holy Spirit," the challenge

[3] Henry Sloan Coffin, *Some Christian Convictions*, p. 145.
[4] *Ibid.*, p. 147.
[5] George B. Stevens, *The Christian Doctrine of Salvation*, p. 437. Used by permission of publisher, Charles Scribner's Sons.

30

to uprightness on our part. The work of the Redeemer was not a "fictitious haggling with abstract and fictitious justice. It was Infinite Love going forth to seek and to save the lost. It was the father of the prodigal going in search of his boy. It was the Good Shepherd giving his life for the sheep; not, of course, at the demand of justice, but at the instance of divine love." This is the true vicariousness of love, of sympathy, when exercised either by a noble human being or by the Divine! So the purpose of grace, of forgiveness, is not just the "covering of sin" or the paying of a debt. Grace is not primarily concerned with a man's past; its aim is the re-creation of one who up to this moment has been a sinner, so that from this time forward he may "go, and sin no more." It means the coming of a new heart into the man, the renewing of a right spirit there.

By coming to earth in the form of human flesh God shows his willingness to share the sufferings of men and to help bear their burdens. This is not an arbitrary action on the part of the Creator of the race; it is a true expression of his fatherhood. When we sin against his will, it is no more possible for him than for us to wait to be "propitiated." God acts toward his sinning children just as Jesus said men should do: "If thy brother sin against thee, go, show him his fault . . . : if he hear thee, thou hast gained thy brother." This "sharing thy brother's fault" is the experience called propitiation; it is the means of working atonement; and it is as true and practical in human relationships as in divine, for in both the one great aim and end of action is developing within men a genuine character. When we face the problem of redemption for men about us today, the thought of the Apostle becomes our thought: "God was in Christ, reconciling the world unto himself, not imputing their trespasses

31

unto them; and hath committed unto us the word of reconciliation." "While we were yet sinners," God came into our midst in the life and death of Christ, thus expressing his grace and providing a meeting place between himself and men.

THROUGH FAITH MEN RESPOND

In his declaration, "By the grace of God I am what I am," Paul shows that our response (faith) to grace reveals not only that man is dependent upon God but also that man is *akin* to God. In the consciousness of their own failures men have sometimes allowed these words to be interpreted as meaning man's total inability and helplessness, and so it is reasoned that when "God comes in, man goes out." How different and more confident is the statement by Rufus M. Jones "that the Spirit of God identifies itself with the human me into which it enters and whose life it becomes." [6]

When we remember that Jesus spoke of God as "Father" and of men as the "sons" of God, salvation takes on normally the relation of fellowship. Through the centuries the political relationship of ruler and ruled led men to think of God as a majestic Lord and of men as wholly incapable of becoming godlike in character. In such a state *fellowship* between the two seemed utterly impossible; salvation was then thought of as the result of a substitution of the merit of Jesus Christ in the place of that which was lacking in man. But if men are sons made in the image of God, then determination as to whether they will keep his commandments and enter into fellowship with him seems not only possible but normal to them. This capacity for sonship, which

[6] Rufus M. Jones, *The Double Search*, p. 49. Used by permission of publisher, John C. Winston Co.

God through his grace has given to man, is described in Genesis as the "image of God." By such image we mean "man's capacity to respond gratefully to the divine love that patiently seeks him out, and to show his gratitude for God's patient mercy by exhibiting a similar magnanimity to his neighbors, even though they be his enemies." Such an understanding of the relationship of God and man relieves us of the puzzle which troubled our fathers: how "two natures, pole-wide apart, could be united in one Person, for we now know that divinity and humanity are not pole-wide apart. There is something human in God and something divine in man and they belong together." [7]

SAVED BY GRACE THROUGH FAITH

As is shown by the quality of human character produced in the Middle Ages—when society was characterized by master and servant—it is dangerous to exalt God at the expense of man! That, in John Wesley's judgment, was the error made by Whitefield. Whitefield seized upon the truth involved in *grace,* but left off similar recognition of the second vital element in salvation—*faith.* Dr. Walter Horton has summed it up in these striking words, "Faith in God and faith in man are so interdependent that we cannot utterly despair of man without undermining faith in God, just as we cannot ignore God without undermining faith in man." If we fail to see that the worth of moral achievement is not as real to God as it is costly to man, then we miss anew Jesus' appreciation of the woman who broke the alabaster vase of precious ointment in honor of his burial, or of her who washed his feet with her tears and dried them with the hair of her head.

[7] *Ibid.,* p. 37.

"According to your faith be it unto you" indicates the Master's estimate of man's ability and of man's part in salvation. But just what is meant by "faith"? One definition has it: "Faith is the soul's trustful recognition and acceptance of the divine grace." Another expresses the same truth: "Faith in Christ is an eager desire to be like him; it is the choice of his ideals, a conviction of the truth and value of his type of life. It is the will to do God's will, as Jesus reveals and interprets it." [8] Still another speaks of faith in direct relation to salvation: "Personal trust makes the trusting man righteous in God's sight; . . . it is the attitude which contents the Father's heart."

THE MAN WHO DOES NOT HAVE FAITH

Believing that if we confess our sins God is faithful and just to forgive us our sins and to cleanse us from all unrighteousness, listening to the Master as he says, "Thy faith hath made thee whole," and in everyday human experience finding some men apparently forgiven and whole and certain others of our fellows who are not so, we cannot help saying that evidently man's faith is an essential part in salvation. Believing that God loves all his children and seeing that some men live with the Father on the footing of pardoned sonship and others do not, we conclude that in some real sense this difference between the "saved" and the "lost" is something that is within the men themselves. What then is it that leads God to forgive one but not to forgive the other? This difference between one man and another "must turn upon the extent to which he opens himself to the divine influence which is always there, available in its completeness for every child of God."

[8] George B. Stevens, *The Christian Doctrine of Salvation*, p. 459. Used by permission of publisher, Charles Scribner's Sons.

34

By faith man becomes "in Christ, . . . a new creature." We realize that faith alone does not save man; it is "by grace . . . through faith." God offers man forgiveness, inspiration, and strength; as man accepts that offer, he becomes one with God. When the man who has been going contrary to right-eousness turns about—chooses the way and ideals of Christ—then God deals with him as being "in Christ," and in his unity with Christ there dwells the secret power and promise of a holy life. As one thus sets out on the new way of life, God accepts him and treats him as he now *is*, not as what heretofore he has been. This is what is meant by "justification by faith." In the eyes of God the measure of the man is not simply his *past* performance; there is possible for him a *future* performance, and what he is to do and be in the future is causally related to the desire by which he now governs his life. The exercise of faith in the beginning is the entrance upon such a career; and that same ideal, set forth in Jesus Christ, will need to be followed to the end. So the attainment of righteousness in conduct and character is a never-ending process.

The goal of Christian growth and effort may be yet far away for the Christian man; but . . . if he has deliberately chosen it and set his heart upon it, it is by anticipation his . . . and no matter how far he may be from it to-day, he shall reach it if he presses steadily on. . . . Faith is no arbitrary condition of salvation; it is the only conceivable condition of a real attainment of Godlikeness. It is a choice, an aspiration, a yearning for the good and the true, which opens the Kingdom of heaven to men. No spiritual good can be ours until we desire it; nor will any be withheld from us which through appreciation and preference we are capable of receiving.[9]

[9] *Ibid.,* p. 459.

35

Why were the prodigal's return and confession regarded by his father as sufficient to warrant a cordial reception? Certainly not because they took away the sad fact of his foolish spending of his fortune, the humiliation his father had suffered through that experience, or that by this return he was now all that a dutiful son should be. But alongside the reality of the past stood the possible reality of the future, and this attitude of repentance—of trust—was and remains the means of ceasing to be what one is and of becoming that which he may yet be. Jesus told the story; it is the way of life for everyone who will exercise such faith.

GOD AND MEN ACTING TOGETHER

We have seen how God in Christ enters into human life, identifies himself with us, and reveals the energy of grace. But we cannot stop with what has been done for us by someone outside us. Sin is not thrust upon us by some other; it is the result of personal choice. So, too, is salvation. It cannot be a transaction in some realm separate from the individual himself and from his own earnest share in it. Salvation must be a positive winning of the will. A dynamic faith within the man must co-operate with the help that is offered by God. *"Something comes down from above, but something must also go up from below."* [10] Paul, who has given the most vital interpretation of both sides of the truth of redemption, uses the word "faith" to name the human part of the process. There is no easy road out of a sinful nature into a holy nature. It is vain to try to patch up a scheme which will relieve us of our share of the tragedy of sin.

[10] Rufus M. Jones, *The Double Search*, p. 79. Used by permission of publisher, John C. Winston Co.

As a man soweth, so also shall he reap. Because we have sinned, we suffer; it cannot be escaped. But because the Redeemer is willing to suffer with us, he makes his appeal of love to us to share his life as he shares ours. "It is not repeating his words that saves us, it is re-living his life, co-dying, and co-rising with him, and entering with a radiant joy, caught from his face, into the common task of redeeming a world of sin to a kingdom of love and holiness." [11]

Note

If it is true that grace *and* faith are the essential factors in salvation, if it is true that God moves directly upon the hearts of men by the Holy Spirit and indirectly through the Word and the sacraments as preached and administered in "the church, which is his body," then every definition and use of Word and sacrament employed by the Church in promoting salvation must be made in harmony with the reality and the exercise of grace and faith.

In the chapters below the assumption is followed that Jesus said: "Go ye into all the world, and preach;" "this do in remembrance of me." Here, then, are two means—preaching and the sacraments—of bringing the fact of the grace of God to consciousness in men and of arousing men to faith. For some individuals, and in some phases of its application, the grace of God can be promulgated with greatest efficiency by preaching; Peter's preaching on the Day of Pentecost is an example. However great Paul's appreciation of the Lord's Supper may have been, surely he relied much upon the spoken—and the written—word as a means of calling men to God. There are other men who come to God

[11] *Ibid.,* p. 81.

more perfectly by participating in the sacraments; so for them preaching is secondary in importance. Our Protestant inheritance would incline us to use both agencies and to believe that the God who is held before men in the spoken word of the sermon is the same God who is offered to humankind by the "elevation of the Host." And further, that the psychological principle upon which the sacraments "work" is the same principle upon which they who "hear" are led to believe.

Means of Grace

IF MEN are saved "by grace ... through faith," then the great task of the Church is to bring to consciousness in men this grace, this lovingkindness of God, as revealed in Christ Jesus and so to arouse in them that response which we call "saving faith." In the first days after the ascension of our Lord, when "the church, which is his body" was beginning to realize its obligation, Paul declared to the Romans: "Brethren, my heart's desire and prayer to God for Israel is, that they might be saved. ... The word is nigh thee ... that if thou shalt confess with thy mouth the Lord Jesus, ... thou shalt be saved. ... For whosoever shall call upon the name of the Lord shall be saved." But then Paul asked the question, apt in that day and in ours, "How then shall they call on him in whom they have not believed? and how shall they believe in him of whom they have not heard? and how shall they hear without a preacher?"

Seventeen hundred years later "the church, which is his body" was under the same responsibility, and men in that day who had need of salvation were asking the same questions. One of them, in writing to Wesley, phrased it, "If you say, Believe, and thou shalt be saved; he answers, True; but how shall I believe? You reply, Wait upon God. Well; but how am I to wait?" For us all Wesley reasoned, in

39

reply, "It cannot possibly be conceived, that the word of God should give no direction in so important a point; or, that the Son of God, who came down from heaven for us men and for our salvation, should have left us undetermined with regard to a question wherein our salvation is so nearly concerned." And with confidence our father in Methodism continued, "In fact, he hath not left us undetermined; he hath showed us the way wherein we should go. We have but to consult the oracles of God." In the conclusion which he drew, based upon scripture, we have the reason for using all the different means of grace common to the Church in all ages, "According to this, according to the decision of Holy Writ, all who desire the grace of God are to wait for it in the *means* which he hath ordained; in using, not in laying them aside."

Included among these means of grace, said Wesley, "are prayer, whether in secret or with the great congregation; searching the Scriptures; and receiving the Lord's Supper . . . and these we believe to be ordained of God, as the ordinary channels of conveying his grace to the souls of men." But lest those who heard and followed his advice might think that means of grace are themselves able to work the works of redemption, Wesley explained the necessity of "faith" in receiving the sacraments:

Settle this in your heart, that the . . . mere work done profiteth nothing; that there is no power to save, but in the spirit of God . . . ; that consequently, even what God ordains, conveys no grace to the soul if you trust not in him alone. . . . Remember also, to use all means, as *means;* as ordained, not for their own sake, but in order to the renewal of your soul in righteousness

40

and true holiness. If, therefore, they actually tend to this, well; but if not, they are dung and dross.

THE MEANING OF "MEANS OF GRACE"

Whatever interpretation may have been given to "means of grace" by the Church through the centuries, or by other denominations today, Methodists sanction the understanding given by Wesley: "By means of grace I understand outward signs, words, or actions, ordained of God, and appointed for this end, to be the ordinary channels whereby he might convey to men, preventing, justifying or sanctifying grace." So wherever that which is physical—a prayer, reading the Scriptures, the use of a ceremony—is employed to *suggest* to the seeking soul the fact of God and his grace, there we find the working of the sacramental principle. It matters not whether it be instruction for teaching, the revelation of will, the arousing of moral energy, or the inducing of an attitude of kindliness or penitence; "that which counts is the fact that in some way and for some purpose that which is physical and material is the instrument of that which is mental and spiritual."

WHY MEN NEED PHYSICAL MEANS OR SACRAMENTS

Man is body as well as spirit. We are not able to explain exactly how our spirits are related to the physical bodies in which we live, but we do realize that in human experience the two together are normal. It is in this physical experience that God comes to man and awakens him where he is. And since it is only in the physical body that we can think, will, and feel, it follows that in the realm of worship "we can hardly dispense with some ritual act, some sensible image [such as prayer or sermon or ceremony] if that act of wor-

41

ship is to turn our humanity in its wholeness toward God." So far as the race has understanding of its experience, the soul receives its impressions and performs its actions by means of the body. It was so when Jesus spoke, saying, "Ye are witnesses." "Inasmuch as ye have done it unto one of the least of these my brethren, ye have done it unto me." To Paul likewise the physical was the means of promoting the spiritual: "Know ye not that ye are the temple of God?"

SPIRITUAL TRUTH EXPRESSED IN PHYSICAL FORM

If truth is to be recognized by the human being—himself body as well as spirit—then truth must come to him in physical form. This is the case in nature as well as in religion. The beauty of a painting, the majesty of a towering peak, and the serenity of a sunset never come most completely to consciousness in human thought in the abstract but always in embodied substance. So when God made the perfect manifestation of himself, he came to earth in the physical body of a human being. The life, teaching, and death of Jesus were appropriate expressions of God's love for mankind. The Church needs something that is external in order to express and stimulate the inward spirit. The Almighty might have *declared*, truthfully and completely, "God so loved the world"; but apparently in his infinite understanding he realized that if his finite creatures were ever to comprehend the reality of that love, it would need to be expressed in the physical body of his Son on the cross. It is in the use of the physical that men normally grasp the spiritual; and it is upon this principle that the minister reads the Scriptures to the congregation, preaches a sermon, and administers the sacrament. In the first case it is the printed page, in the second it is the spoken word, and in the third

42

it is the use of bread and wine to suggest to worshipers the
fact of the love of God.

Since men are as truly physical as they are spiritual, it is
normal that even in their innermost experiences they find
need of rites as well as of words. The history of the race
confirms that judgment. In every age there have been those
souls who have run away from the group to find in solitude
their nearest approach to divinity. For such persons it may
be that both words and signs are a hindrance. But these
persons are individualists of an unusual type; and although
they should not be compelled to follow modes of worship
unnatural to them, it would be equally improper to deny
to the greater proportion of their brethren the use of those
means which are of genuine assistance. Evil is not most
destructive when it has to do with the physical alone, nor
does religion come into its purest state when the body
is kept completely "under." Religion is for the whole person,
physical and spiritual, and that man is most holy who relates
body and soul according to the design of him who created
us. We need the language of reason, as precise and as full
as it can be made; we need the language of art, which trans-
ports the mind into regions of the depth and height of truth;
and we need the language of action, like a hand pointing to
the distance where vision fails, "like a hand held behind the
ear in the consciousness of a music whose vibrations are
barely audible." Abraham, Isaiah, Paul, and Martin Luther
did not all worship in exactly the same way, yet each worshiped truly. Each made use of physical means through
which he endeavored to "please God." Of course mistakes
have been made, and there are times when the form has
ceased to embody the power of godliness; but the mistakes
which have thus crept into the ceremonies of religion have

not nullified the principle of the value of Word and sacrament.

MEANS OF GRACE HELP THE WORSHIPER BECOME AWARE OF GOD

The usefulness of the sacraments depends "upon their inherent nature as rites adapted to illustrate the truths of the Gospel." In this way means of grace become teaching agencies, object lessons, through which we gain understanding necessary to our appreciation of God. Through suggestion made by the means used in this normal way, the attention of the worshiper may be directed to the ideas held in mind by the leader of the service. The principle followed here is that the offered idea has opportunity for consideration in the measure in which the mind of the worshiper is at that moment at ease. For example, before the service opens persons in the congregation are often engaged in conversation; then the organ sounds out its note of call to worship. In the measure in which people turn their attention from what has been engaging their minds and begin to think upon those things which are pure and worthy and of good report, the qualities upon which they meditate begin to become a part of the worshipers themselves. So the effectiveness of whatever means may be employed is in proportion (1) to its ability to lead men to cease thinking upon that with which they are engaged, and (2) to its ability to make forceful suggestion of the new ideas held before them.

"Wherever an omnipresent God is specially realized, he specially is." It is in accord with this principle that the *real* presence of Christ appears to worshipers at the Lord's Supper. It is because "the whole rite is charged with the association of his personality. The words, the elements, the

44

acts carry us back directly to the supreme crisis of his life. No man can be present at the rite with a serious purpose without thinking vividly of him." And to think earnestly of Jesus Christ is to realize his presence, to be with him, to open the heart to all the influence which comes from contact with his Spirit, and to be in him and he in us.

THE SERMON COMPARED TO SACRAMENTS AS MEANS OF GRACE

First of all, let us keep in mind that "by grace are ye saved through faith;" and secondly, that the revelation of this "good news" through Jesus Christ is what we call the gospel. Furthermore, by "means of grace" we understand those outward agencies by which this historic revelation of God in Christ is brought to the attention of men for their salvation. The gospel is this good news, and the agencies employed to persuade men to accept that good news are "means of grace." This good news is "preserved in the Scriptures, preached by the living voice, pictured in the sacraments, and progressively verified in Christian experience."

Here different opinions have been held through the centuries. In his opposition to some phases of teaching and practice in the Church, Luther made appeal directly to the Scriptures. Since Luther's day Protestants have continued that wide use of the Bible, and so from Sunday to Sunday throughout the world Protestant ministers stand before congregations to expound and apply the truth of the Scriptures. Thus the preacher endeavors to lead his people into consciousness of God. It is assumed that men, having been created by the Almighty, are capable of some measure

45

of direct experience with God; and so in the sermon the truth of God is made vivid, concrete, and personal. It is also through the sermon that the will is most directly addressed and men are led to that consecration of self which is the truest worship.

Another emphasis is made by Roman Catholic churches. All churches use both sermon and sacrament, but Catholic thought views the sermon as working upon one principle and the sacraments upon another. Take this explanation, for example, from the Anglican point of view:

And here, precisely, lies the ground of the distinction which we make between communion with Christ through the ministry of the Sacrament and communion through the ministry of the Word (i.e. in preaching or exhortation). That the latter is a real means of communion with Christ we do not for one moment question. But we do not feel it wrong to measure (roughly and fallibly no doubt) what we have received through the ministry of the Word by the immediate effects produced within our consciousness. If we feel unenlightened or unmoved by the word of exhortation, even though we tried to dispose ourselves rightly to receive it, then we conclude (perhaps owing to some defect in us) the ministry has on this occasion been relatively ineffective. But we dare not so judge concerning the efficacy of the Sacrament. Although, then, the grace of communion offered in both cases be the same, yet the manner of its offering and reception is different. In the case of the Sacrament, if we approach with humble and sincere intention, we may rely absolutely on the thing done in accordance with Christ's institution, no matter how dull our own feelings, nor how unworthy the minister. In the case of the Word, our own feelings and understandings on the one hand, and the personal fitness of the minister on the other, must enter much more largely into the account.[1]

[1] Roderick Dunkerly, *The Ministry and the Sacraments*, pp. 135-36. Used by permission of publisher, Student Christian Movement Press.

The Methodist understanding is that what is offered in the sermon is exactly the same as what is offered in the sacrament—the good news of God's love revealed through Jesus Christ! This gospel is expressed in the inspired word which we call the Bible. This same gospel is portrayed in the Sacrament of the Lord's Supper and so is available to the worshiper upon the *same condition* in the sacrament as in the sermon. But if the preacher gives a poor exposition of the Scriptures, or if the priest bungles the administration of the rites, then the worshiper is in corresponding measure handicapped in gaining what otherwise he might have received in that service. And furthermore, however clear may be the explanation of scripture teaching, and however worthy may be the administration of the sacrament, if the mind of the worshiper either is unworthy or is occupied with other matters during that service, he carries away with him little of the grace there offered. God is always anxious to bestow his grace; every minister truly called to his holy task, and intent in his heart upon being a witness for the Almighty, endeavors to serve effectively in word and in sacrament. But preacher and priest alike realize that God gives to the soul only that grace which the soul is spiritually capable of receiving. The whole method of work and teaching employed by the Master requires some measure of co-operation from those whom he seeks to help. Whether the agency in hand is the Sermon on the Mount or the Last Supper in the upper room, the principle is the same: "He that hath, to him shall be given"; "seek and ye shall find"; "according to your faith be it unto you." However abundant be God's grace—offered in sacrament or in sermon—man profits nothing thereby unless he exercises faith.

47

4.

The Lord's Supper

For I have received of the Lord that which also I delivered unto you, That the Lord Jesus the same night in which he was betrayed took bread: and when he had given thanks, he brake it, and said, Take, eat: this is my body, which is broken for you: this do in remembrance of me.

After the same manner also he took the cup, when he had supped, saying, This cup is the new testament in my blood: this do ye, as oft as ye drink it, in remembrance of me. For as often as ye eat this bread, and drink this cup, ye do shew the Lord's death till he come.

TERMS USED IN CONNECTION WITH THE LORD'S SUPPER

THE NAME which is probably used most frequently among Methodists for this service is the *Sacrament*. This is not a scriptural title, but one which came into use by Christians very early in the Roman Empire. Some writers believe it entered Christian terminology just after A.D. 100, largely through the influence of Pliny. Much criticism was being made against the Christians, and persecution was breaking out here and there; so Emperor Trajan sent Pliny out to make investigation and bring back information upon which he might base a policy of dealing with this religious group. Pliny explained to the emperor that the Christians were accustomed to assemble on a fixed day before daybreak and sing a hymn to Christ as a god, and that they bound themselves with an oath not to do any wrong. He continued, "After these things were done, it was their custom to depart and to meet together again to take food, but ordinary and harmless food." Though varying somewhat from its earlier meaning, the Latin word translated into the English "sacrament" seems to have centered upon the pledge, or oath, which the Christians took together.

A second term associated with this rite is that of *Communion*. Apparently it grew out of the sense of brotherhood enjoyed by Christians in that early day. Paul speaks of "the cup of blessing which we bless, is it not the communion of the blood of Christ?" And then concerning the other element employed, "For we being many are one bread, and one body: for we are all partakers of that one bread." This conception is particularly apt among those bodies in which it is the custom to come and kneel together while receiving the elements.

Like *Sacrament*, the *Lord's Supper* comes out of the usage of the early Church rather than from the Bible. This third term is based of course upon the meeting of Jesus with his disciples in the upper room. A meal served at that time of day commonly has been called "supper," and, since he who was the host to the Twelve was believed by them to be "Lord," such a name is normal.

A fourth name used among Anglicans and Roman Catholics is *Eucharist*. It is based upon the passage, "He took the cup, and gave thanks." One writer comments: "Perhaps it would add to the immediate quickening of interest in the Sacrament if this note of triumph were sounded more constantly in our Communion meditation and our hymns."[1]

[1] Hugh Thomson Kerr, *The Christian Sacraments* (Westminster Press, 1944), p. 94. Used by permission.

49

Catholics use still another name, *The Mass*. A custom among early Methodists was that all who desired to attend their worship services were welcome, but after the general meeting was concluded, the members of the society would gather to discuss more intimately matters of personal religious experience. Similarly among early Catholics, visitors, catechumen (probationers), members—all would come to the public service. When the general service was over, the priest would say, "*Ite missa est*"—"Go now, the congregation is dismissed." Thereafter the formal Sacrament of the Lord's Supper would be held. Through custom Mass has come to be the name of the service, and there are masses of many kinds, depending upon the particular interest to be emphasized. In Catholic understanding the distinctive character of all such services is the teaching that the flesh and blood of the crucified One are present there together with the soul and divinity of Jesus Christ. TRANSUBSTANTIATION.

MAJOR EMPHASES IN THE LORD'S SUPPER

In the sermon are offered instruction, conviction, and inspiration. As men listen and meditate, their souls share in genuine worship. Although there are other truths included in the Holy Communion, five major emphases have been made in this service:

1. It is a memorial. When Jesus said, "This do in remembrance of me," he was not only recommending a means of spiritual renewal but was also representing the experience of men at their best. When a family has lost its head, or a group of friends its leader, how natural that they should recall his last words, think of his last wishes, and feel the presence of his spirit with them! So the Lord's Supper bids us remember the supreme experience of Jesus Christ, and the

50

mind of the worshiper goes back to "Bethlehem and its manger, Nazareth and the carpenter's shop, Capernaum and its miracles of healing, Samaria and its well, Jerusalem with its hosannas, and its Upper Room." [2] Such remembrance binds men to their past, to the highest and best of their past!

> According to Thy gracious word,
>   In meek humility,
> This will I do, my dying Lord,
>   I will remember Thee.
>
> Thy body, broken for my sake,
>   My bread from heaven shall be;
> Thy testamental cup I take,
>   And thus remember Thee.
>
> Remember Thee, and all Thy pains,
>   And all Thy love to me;
> Yea, while a breath, a pulse remains,
>   Will I remember Thee!
>
> And when these failing lips grow dumb,
>   And mind and memory flee,
> When Thou shalt in Thy kingdom come,
>   Then, Lord, remember me!

2. It is a communion. The word "communion" is taken over directly from the New Testament. "The cup of blessing which we bless, is it not a communion of the blood of Christ?" "In communion two personalities give themselves, and their thoughts, and feelings, and hopes, and loves, to each other." [3] We have the same sense of oneness with the

---

[2] W. M. Clow, *The Church and the Sacraments*, p. 245. Used by permission of publisher, James Clarke & Co., Ltd.

[3] *Ibid.*, p. 246.

51

Lord in those hours when our faith and love are in flood tide. Under opposite circumstances it is true that

multitudes of believing men will agree that they have had as close and as uplifting communion with Christ, in some lonely hour, when they were far from the voices of men, or in some time of sickness and weakness and outcasting, or in the fellowship of some other believer, with whom they walked by the way. But as we mingle with men on the broad highway, as the cares of this life afflict us, as we find the world too much with us and we lay waste our souls, or when the fire of devotion burns low, and the eternal certainties grow dim, or when some ashaming sin has darkened our mind and chilled our spirit, then, to pass into the Lord's Supper, and to find all the evidence and suggestion of its symbols making their appeal, is to know that communion of the body and blood which gives faith its victory.[4]

The Second Helvetic Confession exhorts: "The Lord's Supper reminds us that we are members of his body, and should live peaceably with all our brethren, and grow and persevere in holiness."

3. It is a "showing forth," a proclaiming that Jesus is Lord. Coming near to the end of his "Life of Jesus," the author of the Fourth Gospel explains, "These are written, that ye might believe that Jesus is the Christ, the Son of God; and that believing ye might have life through his name." That is also Paul's conception: "As often as ye eat this bread, and drink this cup, ye do shew the Lord's death." The Goodspeed translation has it: "For until the Lord comes back, every time you eat this bread and drink from the cup, you proclaim his death." The human race has been greatly inspired by the example which Jesus set in dealing with his fellow men; social reform based upon his

John
Paul

[4] *Ibid.*, pp. 246-47.

52

teachings has done away with human slavery, taught men to regard their fellows, and insisted that nations are, like individuals, subject to the laws of justice and right. But the Lord's Supper voices the idea that that example and those teachings are not enough! The death of Jesus Christ on the cross was the one full and complete manifestation of the grace of God. "God was in Christ, reconciling the world unto himself." Every time his followers participate in the Sacrament of the Lord's Supper they proclaim anew, they show forth that truth.

4. It is an anticipation of his "coming again" and of our achieving his likeness. "Ye do shew the Lord's death until he come." Oftentimes men have placed such a calendar emphasis upon "until he come" as to overlook the real objective of the Master. Let one read the statement of Jesus: "Verily I say unto you, I shall no more drink of the fruit of the vine, until that day when I drink it new in the kingdom of God." With what confidence he seems to have spoken these words!

The Kingdom of God had been Christ's highest earthly purpose. It was the rule and realm of God in the hearts and lives of men—that transcendent life in which all the hopes and longings of earth and time shall be fulfilled, and those who know Christ will enter into a closer intimacy with Him, as He will with them, in a realm where "there shall be no more death." . . . We do not know all the breadth and depth of Christ's words. They are too high for us. . . . But, as often as we eat this bread and drink this cup, the solemn certainties of the living Redeemer, the assurance of His spiritual personality, and the conviction of a quickened faith that He will manifest Himself in a way that will fulfil His drinking of the fruit of the vine in an experience yet to come, are made sure.[5]

[5] *Ibid.*, p. 248.

HOW THE LORD'S SUPPER AIDS THE WORSHIPER

1. *It provides a framework of worship*. Worship seems to be normal in human beings. Everyone finds satisfaction in offering praise to and in adoring those whom he loves. This adoration and praise, directed toward God, we call worship. In order that such thanksgiving and meditation may be exercised most helpfully, there seems to be needed some commonly approved and followed plan. Although one star differs from another, and each individual in some sense is unlike all his fellows, there is a common element in all stars and in all persons; and one of the real joys of life is in the realization that one is in conformity with those of his group, that the manner in which one acts is approved by his friends. This craving for ordered self-expression is deep-rooted, and the measure in which sacraments furnish a framework within which one may have unity with his brethren in this highest act of humankind marks the service which that agency provides.

2. *The ritual, bread, and wine are physical means through which the spirit of worship may be exercised*. Through the words of the ritual the minister speaks to earnest souls, guiding them in their meditation. And then when words can no longer express the reality in contemplation, he directs them through elements of bread and wine. In Christian tradition bread and wine are natural symbols of the life of God and man, of common human needs and their supply, of God's blessing upon human aspirations and endeavor. Bread broken and wine shared are natural tokens of a life received from and consecrated to God, spent in feeding the hungry, surrendered even unto death for the salvation of others. As in the mind of the worshiper these physical emblems become

54

associated with the divine life, they are to that worshiper genuine means of grace.)These words and elements and acts are alive with the personality of Jesus Christ. Other elements would not be equally effective simply because they are not equally symbolic of and charged with the idea of the "broken body and the shed blood" of the Lord.

3. The whole ceremony *suggests* Jesus to the worshiper. The Lord's Supper holds before the mind of the worshiper the image and words of Jesus. As one writer has explained it, "The Holy Communion is like a letter which by means of ink and paper brings to us the will, the counsel, and the affection of our friend." The words of the letter are not our friend, but they do suggest our friend to us, and they do present for our consideration his ideas and ideals. Whether any benefit is received by us through the presence of the letter and the ideals there indicated depends upon our understanding of our friend's ideas and the use which we make of them. If the letter is written in a language which we do not understand, then, although we might assume that the writer sent it because he desired our good, we still would not know exactly what he was endeavoring to convey in the letter. If we come to understand the words of the letter and are willing to follow the advice there given, the good desired by our friend for us becomes a reality in our experience.

We believe that Jesus lived, taught, and died to help men to realize the love of God for all mankind. We break the bread and pour the wine as symbols of the physical experiences of the Master, marking the significance of his action on our behalf. The remembrance of him, renewed by the bread and the wine, helps us to fulfill the commandment which shall change the kingdoms of the world into the kingdom of God: "That ye love one another; even as I have loved you."

It tends to produce quietness of mind in the worshiper and to offer themes for meditation. All ceremonies of the Church are ordered upon the principle that effectiveness in a service depends upon the attention the worshiper gives to the ideal set forth in the service. People come into the sanctuary direct from participation in the normal activities of life. It is desired that here they "think upon things which are holy." And so the whole program is planned to help them drop from attention all other concerns and to bring to thought "the one thing needful." To that end are employed music and scripture and prayer and sermon and sacrament. Following the assumption that "the more the energy of the mind is being expended upon what it of itself wills to think or to do, the less it is open to suggestion; the more its initiative energy is suspended, the more it experiences the force of suggestion," the ritual is so arranged as to free the minds of the worshipers from subjects with which they are concerned and to place before them the themes inherent in the gospel. The music, the scripture, moments of silence—all are admirably shaped to produce a state of mind forgetful of all else and expectant toward the aim of the ceremony. Whatever burden of sin is upon the worshiper's mind is laid aside by confession; its anxieties are allayed by intercession and thanksgiving; the act of giving and receiving the bread and the wine suggests the increase of strength which passes from the Source of all life to the life of the trusting soul. And so the worshiper tends to become one with Christ Jesus.

The Lord's Supper leads to action on the part of the worshiper. The service calls upon us to do something for ourselves. In other forms of worship "we are read to, we are preached to, we are sung to, we are prayed for." More directly than is true in other acts of worship, the Lord's Supper calls upon us to examine our lives; "to make definite confession to God for definite sins; to make definite acts of penitence, of resolution, of self-dedication; and to make open confession before our fellow men of our desire to lead the life of Christ."

The Lord's Supper induces a sense of brotherhood. The earnest communicant comes to the table of the Lord upon invitation of the minister: "Ye that do truly and earnestly repent of your sins, and are in love and charity with your neighbors . . . draw near with faith." More than any other service the Holy Communion helps us to realize the idea of the Christian society. It was within the fellowship of the Twelve that the Master instituted this sacrament; for them, and for all the family of God in which he was a Son, Jesus was about to go to the cross. "Inasmuch as ye have done it unto one of the least of these," he said, and equally he had affirmed the truth, "He that loveth not his brother loveth not God." Kneeling at the Lord's table we realize anew the unity of the whole human race in the sight of the heavenly Father!

CONDITIONS FOR ADMISSION TO THE LORD'S SUPPER

1. In the days of the early Christian Church, about the middle of the second century a minister by the name of Justin addressed a letter to the emperor at Rome. Christians were being persecuted bitterly, and Justin believed that if the emperor really understood the Church, its teachings and customs, he would not think of it as a dangerous organization and so would not oppose its members. Justin drew up

and addressed to the emperor what has been called his "Apology." It was a straightforward exposition of Christian doctrine and ceremony.

When he came to explain to this representative of the State the practice of the Lord's Supper and upon what condition one might be admitted to that ceremony, he said: "All those who believe what we teach to be true and will promise to endeavor to live in accordance with these ideals are welcome to share in this service." That probably is about as representative a statement of the early Church as could be found.

The emperor was not convinced; persecution did not cease. And tradition tells us that when the officers of state ordered Justin to surrender his faith or give up his life, he laid his head upon the block. Biographers of him who issued invitation to the Holy Communion upon condition of belief in the Lord Jesus and the keeping of his commandments call that man Justin Martyr!

2. As the Christian Church spread over the empire and its new members came increasingly from among those whose almost every act of life was controlled by specific legislation, the Church lost its earlier freedom, and its services were hedged about by rigid regulation. Within one hundred years after the martyrdom of Justin, Cyprian— Bishop of Carthage—had given utterance to what became a classic: "He who does not have the Church for his mother cannot have God for his Father." Before another hundred years baptism had taken on the function of regeneration, and Christians spoke of the elements of the Lord's Supper as the flesh and blood of the Lord Jesus. To such a people of course membership in the Church would be an indispensable condition to participation in the Lord's Supper. Such

regulation exists in the Roman Catholic Church to this day.

3. One of the most striking conditions for admission to the Lord's Supper among our Protestant churches in America today is that of the Southern Baptists. It is what is called "close Communion." A century ago that custom was observed generally among Baptists, but in more recent years it has frequently been relaxed by those living north of the Mason-Dixon line.

"Close Communion" among Baptists has sometimes operated upon the assumption that to enjoy the privilege of the Lord's Supper one must not only be a Baptist, but his membership must be held in the congregation in which that service is observed. Members of a Baptist church in town A, worshiping with friends in town B, would not be expected to take Communion with their brethren in this second congregation.

To many that custom seems strange. But no practice should be condemned until one knows the convictions upon which it rests. And before Baptists are singled out as different from others of our religious bodies, let it be remembered that before the American Revolution no prominent denomination in all the world had ever practiced "open Communion." Until after the adoption of the Constitution of the United States, every major Christian body followed the rule of "close Communion." "Open Communion" is a product of our American democratic way of life; it has come out of the idea of freedom of thought and speech and worship. And throughout the world only in those countries characterized in their common life by such democracy is the Holy Communion available to persons not members of the specific group providing that means of grace.

Close Communion deserves another word. If one asks

59

an informed member among the Baptists why they have set up such a rule, that one probably will reply, and with confidence: "Baptists do not make the rules concerning the Lord's Supper; Jesus made them; and Baptists simply try to follow his commands." That is the interpretation of the New Testament honestly held by millions in this, one of the largest and most wholesomely influential denominations in America.

Jesus understood that evening when in the upper room he gathered about him his most intimate followers that there were at that hour many—within convenient walking distance—who loved him so truly that they would die for him. In his understanding, Baptists would say, this ceremony is not for general observance, but to be shared only by those most intimately associated in religious matters. It is for the members of a local congregation; every true congregation, or "church," of believers in Jesus Christ is to have the joy of participation in the Lord's Supper but only within the fellowship of their brethren in that local body.

Methodists had something like this in their early societies. In the general worship service held by the Methodists all people who desired to come and to share were welcome. But when that public assembly had been dismissed, the members of the little society gathered for the more intimate experience of prayer and testimony. In that service, more searching and meaningful than could be possible with strangers present, our fathers joined to the strengthening of their souls. One of the rules, adopted early and carried long in Methodist custom, was that a person might not attend the society meeting more than twice or three times unless he joined.

However we may differ from the Baptists in our interpretation of the New Testament in its rules for admission to the Table of the Lord, like them we believe that every person has the right to read the Bible for himself and to follow that Book as he understands its teachings. Therefore surely no Methodist would criticize a Baptist for his honest following of the concept of "close Communion." Rather would we say, "The Lord bless you in the study of his word and in the doing of his will!"

4. When asked upon what condition he admitted persons to the Sacrament of the Lord's Supper, Mr. Wesley answered: "I invite to the Table of the Lord every person whom I invite to the Lord, and upon the same condition: 'Ye that do truly and earnestly repent of your sins.'" As Methodists understand, he is Lord of all who put their trust in him, whether they are gathered in the fold of Methodist, Baptist, Roman Catholic, or other; he is the Host, and at his table all who need strength may find it there. His invitation is "whosoever will"; his exhortation pleads: "Come unto me, all ye that labour and are heavy laden, and I will give you rest." The only condition is the willingness to come, the turning away from sin, and the walking in the paths of righteousness. This attitude of Jesus in the Lord's Supper is like that of the prophets in their preaching of the mind of Jehovah as welcoming to his bounties men not only of the Jewish race but of all tribes and peoples: "Ho, every one that thirsteth, come ye to the waters, and he that hath no money; come ye, buy, and eat; yea, come, buy wine and milk without money and without price." In another figure the Scriptures again present this universal welcome of the Almighty. The New Jerusalem, the holy city of God, is represented as enclosed with a wall having twelve gates—three on the north, three on the south, three on the east, and three on

61

the west. Earnest men of every temperament—the deeply emotional, those of more analytical disposition, the rich, the poor, the aristocratic, and the lowborn—are equally members of the family of God. The Father loves and welcomes them all if only they have "a desire to flee from the wrath to come and to be saved from their sins." To his ministers Jesus said, in parable, "Go out into the highways and hedges, and compel them to come in, that my house may be filled." Methodists relate their doctrine of the Lord's Supper to this instruction of Jesus.

Another modification John Wesley made in the common understanding of the relation of men to the Lord's Supper is that not only are all men who are invited to the Lord invited to his table, and upon the same condition, but also repentant souls may find their Lord for the first time while kneeling at that table. "My brother and I," said Mr. Wesley, "used to preach that the Lord's Supper is a 'confirming' ordinance, designed for the strengthening of the faith of those who are already believers; but now we know that the Holy Communion may be a 'converting' as well as a confirming ordinance." In imagination one may behold him there, preaching on the hillside and pointing his finger at the multitudes as he declared: "Many now within the sound of my voice know the beginning of your conversion came while you were kneeling at the Holy Communion."

In the great revival meetings of the nineteenth century here in America one of the distinctive provisions of every campground was the "mourners' bench." When the preacher had finished his earnest sermon, appealing to men to repent of their sins and turn unto God, he would urge sinners to come and kneel at the mourners' bench in search of the conscious experience of the forgiveness of their sins. Upon what condition would the evangelist invite these men to accept Jesus Christ as Saviour? Upon the identical condition that our ritual today invites persons to the Lord's Supper: "Ye that do truly and earnestly repent of your sins." Mrs. Wesley confirmed her son John in that view when she testified: "While I was kneeling at the Lord's Supper, receiving the elements at the hands of my son-in-law Wesley Hall, the Lord gave me assurance that for Christ's sake he had taken away all my sins." Everyone, old in the service of the Master or just entering into that service, needs that refreshing, encouraging assurance of the cleansing from all sins; and Methodists have come to look forward with confidence to just such renewal as they kneel humbly at the Lord's table.

Methodists believe this service is for those who have been failing along the way, just as it is intended for those who have achieved "perfection" in their Christian experience. Upon occasion men wrote to Mr. Wesley, quoting Paul's words about eating and drinking damnation. To one in person, and to all in principle, our father in Methodism replied, "I am afraid you have allowed the *sound* of words to deceive you." And then he launched out in his explanation that men farthest away from God are the very ones who have need of that which may be gained as they "draw near with faith, and take this holy Sacrament to your comfort; and devoutly kneeling make your humble confession to Almighty God." Like every other provision of our Lord, those who have greatest need are most surely welcome. The Lord's Supper, then, as understood by Methodists is not only for saints but for all who really want to become saints; and the man who is most keenly conscious of his failures, of his need, certainly meets the condition for a helpful participation in that ceremony.

Still another use of the Lord's Supper has been developing among the Methodists during recent generations. Samuel Wesley left record that he admitted to the Lord's Supper his son John when the boy was about eight and one half years of age, whereas custom in that day was to wait until children were eleven or twelve. The older Wesley explained that he made this exception in the case of John because he believed the boy had reached the stage of moral accountability normal to those of the customary age.

Methodists today take this assumption of Samuel Wesley and both apply and modify it. In the first place, Methodists today do not believe—as did Samuel Wesley—that children are born under the guilt of Adam's sin. And therefore, in the second place, they believe that even young children may be influenced by instruction and association in the realm of religion. In John Wesley's day neither in England nor in America did any community provide schools where *all* children might enjoy free of tuition charge the opportunities of instruction in general education. In religion no such elaborate organization as our church school had ever been undertaken by any denomination. The doctrine of "growth in grace" or of "Christian nurture" was so new to the thinking of those to whom John Wesley preached that when he began to offer them such advantages, the people wondered. Some were interested and asked for further exposition; the more orthodox denounced all such as heresy. But as the Arminian interpretation of the Genesis account—that men are made in the *image of God*—gained ground, more and more the doctrine of growth in his likeness appealed to men as normal. Again and again there was quoted with approval the statement concerning the Master, "And Jesus increased in wisdom and stature, and in favour with God and man." And so today when in the family and in the more formal instruction of church and church school effort has been made to follow the advice of Holy Writ, "Train up a child in the way he should go," thousands of devout, mature saints of the Way stand up and testify, "This day is this scripture fulfilled in your ears."

Methodists believe that one of the ways to "train up a child in the way he should go" is to have him share in the solemn service of the Lord's Supper right along by the side of his parents. Long before young children can "carry a tune," we encourage them to hold the hymnbook with others standing by; years earlier than they are able to grasp the words being sung, or the Scriptures used in response, or the expositions offered in the pulpit, we believe it is for their edification that they share in the service. Under what more inspiring circumstance, where else is to be found more solemn atmosphere, than surrounds the worshipers as they gather at the Lord's table? Surely they do not now understand the hymns, the Scriptures, the ritual; nor do they comprehend spiritually the elements employed; but under what other circumstance may they be able quite so well to *learn*, to *increase* in wisdom and understanding? As soon as little ones are able to conduct themselves so as not to disturb the worship of others gathered there, let them come with their elders to the Holy Communion of the Lord's Supper. Such a conception is coming to be the doctrine of religious education as taught by all our churches.

HOW THE CHURCH THROUGH THE CENTURIES HAS THOUGHT OF THE LORD'S SUPPER

1. The Lord's Supper is Jewish in origin but as used among Christians today is largely Gentile in interpretation. One of the facts that comes to attention in a study of the Lord's Supper is that every great religion in the known history of the world has had some ceremony corresponding to that of the Holy Communion among Christians. No two religions explain God in exactly the same way; the doctrine of man has varied from century to century and as held by different groups in any given period. In the same way the ceremonies which represent the coming together into fellowship of the Maker and his worshipers present many conceptions of the two; but of one blood has the Eternal made all races of men, and investigation shows that in no religious group of them is there lacking some rite in which they break bread and eat together with God. However we may observe or define this universal custom in any group, it binds us all—from all points of geography, all ages of time, all circumstances and stages of civilization—into a kind of universal "communion of saints."

Another striking fact about the history of the Lord's Supper is the exceedingly brief account given of it in the New Testament. No other institution has come to us from the early Church "freighted with such tender associations as that of the Eucharist," yet around no other practice have there been waged such fierce conflicts. In three fourths of Christendom—Greek, Roman, Anglican, and Lutheran—it is believed to be the chief means of grace, the surest and divinest agency for bringing God and all spiritual blessings to the soul. Therefore these churches make it the center of worship; to it all parts of the service lead up, and from it they all lead down. But "over against this," wrote Dr. John A. Faulkner, "notice this fact in the New Testament: the Supper, outside of brief mention of its institution in three Gospels, is clearly mentioned or described in only one place." And again, while "a thousand treatises have been written upon the doctrine of the Supper, the New Testament is almost entirely silent about that doctrine. By careful reading you can make out quite fully from the New Testament the doctrine of God the Father, of Christ, of the Holy Spirit, of sin, regeneration . . . but you can get but little on the doctrine of the Supper."

This is but to say that although the Sacrament of the Lord's Supper was begun in Palestine in the upper room that evening when Jesus gathered about him the Twelve and served them the elements of bread and wine as symbols of his to-be-broken body and shed blood, nearly all the "teachings" we have today about this service and the multitudinous customs which have grown up around it have come out of the Gentile environment into which the Christian Church passed during the late days of the apostles and shortly thereafter.

In this transition from Palestine to Rome there entered the doctrines of the Lord's Supper with which we are now so familiar, and so different are they from the fundamental and prophetic ideals of the former Jewish religion. The Lord's Supper of the Founder of Christianity was a service in which the "pure in heart see God"; the Lord's Supper of the postapostolic and later days was a ceremony reserved for those "who have been duly admitted into the society by certain ritual acts controlled by a sacerdotal succession." In the New Testament forgiveness of sins is conditioned

67

wholly upon repentance and faith; in the church of the Roman Empire absolution might be bestowed only by the priest through formal and elaborate rites characteristic of that Gentile world and known to us today in the Roman Catholic Church.

This does not mean that the Mass of the Roman Catholic Church in the Middle Ages was merely pagan superstition, or that ministry and membership had departed from the truth revealed in Jesus Christ and knew not the God of the fathers. But it does mean that as different as was the worship service of early Christians from that which was followed by their Hebrew ancestors a thousand years before, just so varied also from the ceremonies of the first century were those of the developed Gentile Christian Church. In all these centuries men were honestly endeavoring to come into saving relation to the Almighty, and we believe that Jehovah blesses all who truly call upon his name.

2. The understanding of life common in the Roman Empire at the entry of Christianity was that reality is inherent in physical form. So that when Paul said, "The cup of blessing which we bless, is it not the communion of the blood of Christ? The bread which we break, is it not the communion of the body of Christ?" he would be understood by normal Gentile interpretation as meaning that the bread *is* the flesh and the wine *is* the blood. Some centuries later when the question was raised as to how such a change could be wrought, common explanation came to be that the prayer of the priest was effective for all ordinary benefits; but when that leader provided the Lord's Supper for his people and was about to offer to them the sacred elements, he ceased to employ his own words and delivered

to them these elements in the very words of Jesus himself: "This is my body; this is my blood."

For some hundreds of years there continued differences of opinion upon this idea of the change of the bread into the flesh and the wine into the blood. For example, Ratramnus in the ninth century and Berengarius in the eleventh century could not accept this idea. But shortly all such teaching was officially declared to be heresy; and since the Fourth Lateran Council, in 1215, the denial of transubstantiation is sufficient ground for expulsion from the Roman Catholic Church. During the same general period custom developed that only the bread should be received by the communicants and that the priest should drink the wine on behalf of the members.

With the rise of Protestantism the trend of interpretation concerning the Lord's Supper turned back toward that of the New Testament. Luther took a middle ground. His successors in the Lutheran Church have taught what is called "consubstantiation." Luther denied that the bread is "changed," but he did believe that the flesh of Jesus comes and dwells "with" the bread and the blood of Jesus with the wine. John Calvin, living during the later years of Luther and for a brief space thereafter, thought of the "spiritual flesh and blood" of Jesus as in the bread and wine of the Lord's Supper; whereas Ulrich Zwingli, the Swiss reformer of the same century, taught that the bread and the wine "symbolize," or "represent," the broken body and the shed blood of the crucified Lord. Methodists have been inclined to follow Zwingli, rather than either Luther or Calvin, in this matter. John Wesley observed, "So far as we are able to see the bread and the wine the moment after the prayer of consecration are exactly the same as they were the minute before that invocation was made." That is our teaching today.

In it all, regardless of Catholic or Protestant interpretation, there is great mystery. Although not dealing specifically with bread and flesh, the writer of hymn 112 in the *Methodist Hymnal* has the assurance which is precious to every believer:

> I know not how that Bethlehem's Babe
>   Could in the Godhead be;
> I only know the manger Child
>   Has brought God's life to me.

> I know not how that Calvary's cross
>   A world from sin could free;
> I only know its matchless love
>   Has brought God's love to me.

> I know not how that Joseph's tomb
>   Could solve death's mystery;
> I only know a living Christ,
>   Our immortality.[°]

PREACHING UPON THE LORD'S SUPPER

Concerning the Master it is written, "And he came to Nazareth . . . and, as his custom was, he went into the synagogue. . . . And there was delivered unto him the book of the prophet Esaias. And when he had opened the book, he found the place where it was written, The Spirit of the Lord is upon me, because he hath anointed me to preach the gospel to the poor; he hath sent me to heal the broken-hearted, to preach deliverance to the captives, and recovering

° "Our Christ" by Harry W. Farrington. Used by permission.

of sight to the blind, to set at liberty them that are bruised, to preach the acceptable year of the Lord." There is no "life" of Jesus in the New Testament that does not record him as having emphasized this means of grace called "preaching." One of the last directions given to his followers just before "a cloud took him out of their sight" was, "Go ye into all the world, and preach." The priestly function of worship and the sacraments, valuable indeed in every age, is not by New Testament emphasis to be substituted for solid preaching.

One of the very fruitful phases of preaching in our day is that concerning the sacraments. To the shame of Methodists in our generation is the fact that in many a congregation among us the smallest attendance during the month is that of the service in which the Sacrament of the Lord's Supper is to be observed. That was notorious, too, in the Church of England in Mr. Wesley's day, even among the members of his religious societies. But he was not willing that it should continue to be so. With vigor he set himself to create within his people an appreciation of this great service. He *preached* upon that subject; time and again his *Journal* gives evidence of his doing so. One of his most effective published sermons is upon the subject "The Means of Grace"; another has as its title, "The Duty of Constant Communion." Remembering with what distress he had noted the small numbers attending that worship in his earlier years, and how he had set himself to change that condition, he must have felt great satisfaction as he recorded in his *Journal* concerning a particular "Communion Sunday": "The service began at five o'clock in the morning, and it required six hours to serve the people who came." Upon another occasion he writes, "Those attending were so great in number that we decided to divide them into three groups, having between five and six hundred in each group."

With just such an objective in mind Methodist ministers today should set themselves to frequent and sound preaching upon the sacraments. If one uses the longer section of the ritual as found in the *Methodist Hymnal* today, not much time can be given on that Sunday for preaching. If that is one's custom, then upon other Sundays the minister should deliver a full-length sermon upon some theme which will open to his people the way to a clear and convincing understanding of this means of grace; and sermons of such content and value should be offered with a frequency conducive to a thorough grounding in the meaning and value of the Sacrament of the Lord's Supper. If custom in any pastorate is to employ the briefer form of the ritual, then upon the day of the celebration of the Holy Communion an earnest exposition of ten or twelve minutes may be made to the profit of all who worship there.

In a section entitled "Preaching on the Sacraments" in *The Christian Sacraments*, Dr. Hugh Thomson Kerr lists different themes as profitable:

In the sermons of a long pastorate in the same Church, these sacramental subjects appear: "The Sacramental Evangel"; the text, "This do in remembrance of me." [I Cor. 11:25.] "The World's Greatest Sermon"; the text, "Ye proclaim the Lord's death." [I Cor. 11:26.] . . . "The Guest Chamber"; the text, "Where is my guest-chamber?" [Mark 14:14.] "Christ the Bread of Life"; the text, "I am the bread of life." [John 6:35.] "The Eucharistic Feast"; the text, "When he had given thanks." [I Cor. 11:24.] . . . "Our Lord's Sacramental Claim"; the text, "He that eateth this bread shall live forever." [John 6:51.] . . . "The Guests of God"; the text, "Thou preparest a table before me." [Ps. 23:5.] "The Sacramental Simplicity"; the text, "Come

72

unto me, all ye that labor." [Matt. 11:28.] "The Upper Room"; the text, "Let not your heart be troubled." [John 14:1.] "The Sacramental Invitation"; the text, "Drink ye all of it." [Matt. 26:27.] "Memory and Hope"; the text, "This do . . . till he come." [I Cor. 11:25-26.][7]

Another series of sermons on the Lord's Supper could take as themes ideas suggested in the ritual for the celebration of the Lord's Supper, as follows:

"Ye that do truly and earnestly repent"; theme, Repentance

"In love and charity with your neighbors"; theme, Love for Neighbor

"Intend to lead a new life"; theme, New Life

"Following the commandments of God"; theme, Obedience to God

"Walking . . . in his holy ways"; theme, Living Well Each Day

"Draw near with faith"; theme, Living in the Presence of God

"Take this holy Sacrament to your comfort"; theme, The Comfort of Religion

"Make your humble confession"; theme, Confessing Our Sins

"Meekly kneeling upon your knees"; theme, The Spirit of Humility

Dr. Kerr makes more detailed suggestions for preaching upon the Sacrament of the Lord's Supper by quoting sermon outlines from Alexander Maclaren, Marcus Dods, and James Denney, as follows:

Taking for his text the familiar words, "This do in remembrance of me," Alexander Maclaren begins by stating that the

[7] P. 151 (Westminster Press, 1944). Used by permission.

account of the institution of the Lord's Supper in First Corinthians is older than any of the Gospel records. He divides his sermon, as usual, into three sections: (1) The Lord's Supper is a memorial of the past, and in this part of the sermon the emphasis is on the personal pronoun *me*. (2) It is a symbol for the present. The Christian life is not merely the remembrance of a historical Christ, but the present recognition of a living Christ. (3) It is a prophecy. The emphasis here is on the words, "Til I come." . . .

Dr. Marcus Dods, scholar and preacher, takes the text, "This do in remembrance of me," using the same words for the title. He begins by pointing out our Lord's great simplicity. We are to remember Christ and be thankful. First, it was a kindness to his disciples to give them something to *do*. Secondly, he gave them something to do which would renew their remembrance daily. He chose the symbol of food. Thirdly, he bade them remember him in his death. He desired to be remembered in the hour of his deepest humiliation.

Dr. James Denney has a great sermon on "The Ideal Church"; the text, "They continued stedfastly in the apostles' teaching and fellowship, in the breaking of bread and the prayers." Here are four great themes: The Teaching, The Fellowship, The Breaking of Bread, The Prayers.[8]

When shall the minister preach upon the sacraments? The answer of course must be given by each pastor for himself and his people. The day upon which the observance is held surely offers a challenging opportunity for meditation, for exhortation upon the theme of the sacraments. But probably the best opportunity for instruction, for "giving a reason for the faith that is in you" concerning this most worshipful experience, is upon some day other than that upon which the Communion is held. The most careful planning should be made. Jesus spoke of the "water of life" when a woman came to the well to draw. In one of the editions of the Bible

[8] *Ibid.*, pp. 152-53.

74

a subhead given to Luke, chapter 14, verse 28, is: "What is required of those who would be Christ's disciples?" In the passage the writer is interpreting Jesus as saying to one who would be a disciple of the Lord: "For which of you, intending to build a tower, sitteth not down first, and counteth the cost?" Certainly it would not be a false application of this advice of the Master to say, "And what preacher of you, in taking up the work of his charge for the year, does not sit down and ask himself in the beginning of that year, 'What are some of the truths of the gospel which ought to be expounded before my people this year?'" Andrew W. Blackwood's *Planning a Year's Pulpit Work,* for a while included in the conference course of study, is one of the recent useful books for preachers. Just as normally there come the seasons of autumn, winter, spring, and summer in nature's year, surely there are seasons in the church year which offer superior opportunity for emphasis upon given phases of the gospel. And he who simply waits until Monday morning for the Spirit to suggest to his mind a theme for next Sunday's sermon is missing the larger guidance of inspiration provided by the Almighty through the passing of the seasons of normal spiritual experience. The harvest, or Thanksgiving, season, Christmas and the celebration of Jesus' birth, the weeks leading through Ash Wednesday and Lent up to Holy Week, the Passover and the Crucifixion, Easter and the Resurrection, the weeks up to Pentecost—all are so normally and richly freighted with suggestion for meditation and study of the central themes of the gospel of salvation. How fitting that with these "seasons of refreshing" before him, the minister should "plan a year's pulpit work." And surely within that plan directed at every point —not only from Monday to Sunday but also from season to season—by the conscious guidance of the Holy Spirit, the preacher may speak to his people concerning the sum of gospel truth, the crucifixion, the death, and the resurrection of the Lord; and he may find in the observance of the Lord's Supper a natural, visible sign of that invisible grace.

Concerning the frequency with which the Lord's Supper should be observed—and in similar question, how often the minister should preach upon this general subject—it is believed there is no positive or literal rule. Such would be to fall into the error of the "letter of the law" and so to miss its spirit. Certainly the early Church observed it every Sunday, and that practice was continued until the Protestant Reformation in the sixteenth century. The regular order of the Church of England in the days of John Wesley provided that service always on Sunday, and when Mr. Wesley was making recommendation to the Methodists in America in 1784, he wrote, "And I hope you may observe the Sacrament of the Lord's Supper every Lord's day." Partly because of the long circuits and the inability of the preacher to be present more often than once a month, the observance became less frequent. Frequent Communion was rendered less convenient still by the belief among Methodists that such a service requires an ordained minister, for when our church was organized, only one out of five preachers was ordained. Custom shortly came to be that the Sacrament of the Lord's Supper would be held quarterly when the presiding elder came around. And then, apparently without any thought or design, there grew up among Methodists a constituency who held slight appreciation of this service which reminds us directly of the death of Jesus on our behalf. That is our sad condition today, and to remedy that weakness surely the "planning of a year's pulpit work" should

76

include frequent earnest sermons upon the theme of the significance of the Lord's Supper.

Another suggestion is made, that the service of the Lord's Supper should be a unity. From beginning to end the service should be directed to one central theme. So often ministers mar the occasion by making the observance of the sacrament a mere appendage to an already completed program. Intent upon speaking what he has to say, the preacher seems to forget that this is the Lord's table, that here the Master is present to welcome all who come, and that he has something to *say* to all those who come! The unfolding of some great truth by the preacher is really important in order to prepare the minds of those who are to communicate. But the idea to be presented that day should be so closely related to the general purpose of the Lord's Supper as to lead naturally into its observance, just as in the ritual there is first confession, prayer for cleansing, declaration of praise and adoration, and words of humble access, followed by a prayer that the elements of bread and wine may achieve in the hearts of the worshipers that for which they were intended. "The hymns chosen, the anthems selected, the Scripture read, the sermon preached, should form a complete whole." [9] And above all else:

If, for example, the sermon or Communion meditation has no relation to the cross of Christ, his death and resurrection, then it has no place in such a service. The message of the minister should be the same message as that of the Sacrament, and the eyes of the minister and of his people should be upon the cross, or rather upon him who suffered and triumphed there.[10]

[9] *Ibid.*, pp. 96-97.
[10] *Ibid.*, p. 97.

HYMNS TO BE USED IN THE SERVICE OF THE LORD'S SUPPER

As upon all matters of importance, there is difference of opinion concerning the use of hymns for this service. One view is that just as we employ the same ritual every time we have the Holy Communion, we should also use the same hymns. "In this way they become part of the service itself, and as the years go by a certain significance becomes attached to them. They are kept sacred for the Communion service only and are not used at the regular services." [11] Another view is that, as there are numerous phases of truth included in the Lord's Supper, the hymns employed should be varied. Whichever of these views may be followed, it is certain that the selection of hymns should be made by the minister, and that upon that choosing should be spent much earnest thought long before the hour of celebration. In this the minister should "sit down and count the cost" in his study where, because his mind is not distracted by the presence of other people and the thousand and one interests demanding his attention, the Holy Spirit may have opportunity to guide.

When one ponders upon the major elements of the Communion experience, altogether apart from the preacher's mind or particular appreciation, something of propriety or direction is clear. Because the service is centered upon the Lord, the hymns should be objective rather than subjective. In order to reason rightly about ourselves, first we reason about him who is the source of our being.

> Lord of all being, throned afar,
>   Thy glory flames from sun and star;
> Center and soul of every sphere,
>   Yet to each loving heart how near!

[11] *Ibid.*, p. 101.

78

Our midnight is Thy smile withdrawn;
  Our noontide is Thy gracious dawn;
Our rainbow arch Thy mercy's sign;
  All, save the clouds of sin, are Thine!

Grant us Thy truth to make us free,
  And kindling hearts that burn for Thee,
Till all Thy living altars claim
  One holy light, one heavenly flame.

The following are ten of the many suitable, uplifting, and inspiring hymns in the *Methodist Hymnal*, the tunes for which are familiar to most of our congregations:

"Holy, Holy, Holy! Lord God Almighty" (No. 1), "Praise, My Soul, the King of Heaven" (No. 77), "O God, Our Help in Ages Past" (No. 533), "O Worship the King, All-glorious Above" (No. 4), "The King of Love My Shepherd Is" (No. 353), "The Church's One Foundation" (No. 381), "I Love Thy Kingdom, Lord" (No. 379), "The Lord's My Shepherd" (No. 70), "Crown Him with Many Crowns" (No. 170), and "Spirit of God, Descend upon My Heart" (No. 179).

The second hymn, still objective rather than subjective, should be pointed more specifically at the Cross, and it should express not only contrition but gratitude. It may be called the "Communion hymn." Those named here may prove fruitful at this stage of the service:

"Jesus, Thou Joy of Loving Hearts" (No. 345), "According to Thy Gracious Word" (No. 410), "When I Survey the Wondrous Cross" (No. 148), "Saviour, Thy Dying Love" (No. 219), "Jesus, the Very Thought of Thee" (No. 348), "I Heard the Voice of Jesus Say" (No. 210), and "Just As I Am, Without One Plea" (No. 198).

79

The singing of the hymn "Break Thou the Bread of Life" should be avoided since it refers not to the Sacrament of the Lord's Supper but to the Scriptures.

Oftentimes it may seem best, when all have taken Communion, to close the service simply by asking the congregation to repeat the majestic words of the closing paragraphs of the ritual, Order II:

O Lord, our heavenly Father, we, thy humble servants, desire thy fatherly goodness mercifully to accept this our sacrifice of praise and thanksgiving; most humbly beseeching thee to grant that, by the merits and death of thy Son Jesus Christ, and through faith in his blood, we and thy whole Church may obtain remission of our sins, and all other benefits of his passion. And here we offer and present unto thee, O Lord, ourselves, our souls and bodies, to be a reasonable, holy, and living sacrifice unto thee; humbly beseeching thee that all we who are partakers of this Holy Communion may be filled with thy grace and heavenly benediction. And although we be unworthy, through our manifold sins, to offer unto thee any sacrifice, yet we beseech thee to accept this our bounden duty and service; not weighing our merits, but pardoning our offenses; through Jesus Christ our Lord; by whom, and with whom, in the unity of the Holy Spirit, all honor and glory be unto thee, O Father Almighty, world without end. Amen.

Glory be to God on high, and on earth peace, good will toward men. We praise thee, we bless thee, we worship thee, we glorify thee, we give thanks to thee for thy great glory, O Lord God, heavenly King, God the Father Almighty!

O Lord, the only-begotten Son Jesus Christ; O Lord God, Lamb of God, Son of the Father, that takest away the sins of the world, have mercy upon us. Thou that takest away the sins of the world, have mercy upon us. Thou that takest away the sins of the world, receive our prayer. Thou that sittest at the right hand of God the Father, have mercy upon us. For thou only art holy; thou only art the Lord; Thou only, O Christ, with the Holy Ghost, art most high in the glory of God the Father. Amen.

Upon other occasions, according to the specific phase of truth emphasized by the minister that day, the congregation may best be sent away with the singing of some hymn of consecration or of exultation and thanksgiving. Here follow suitable hymns to express this experience:

"O Jesus, I Have Promised" (No. 226), "O Master, Let Me Walk with Thee" (No. 259), "O Jesus, Thou Art Standing," (No. 197), "Rock of Ages, Cleft for Me" (No. 204), "Jesus Shall Reign Where'er the Sun" (No. 479), "When All Thy Mercies, O My God" (No. 542), "All Hail the Power of Jesus' Name" (No. 164), "O for a Thousand Tongues to Sing" (No. 162), and "Lead On, O King Eternal" (No. 278).

METHODS OF ADMINISTERING THE LORD'S SUPPER

Concerning administration of the Lord's Supper let it be understood throughout the service that wherever persons think intently upon God, there God really is. Since the minister cannot *bestow* salvation upon those who worship there, and since the elements themselves—apart from faith in the soul—are unable to convey salvation to men, the function of the minister is therefore to so guide and direct the thoughts of persons in the service that they may think intently upon God. The ritual for the celebration of the Lord's Supper has been developed through hundreds of years to enable the minister to perform this sacred task. It is in the measure in which he succeeds that he becomes a real priest of the Lord.

This ritual has remained substantially the same throughout the centuries, and though varied somewhat in form, in principle what has proved in experience to be useful at the hands of one denomination has been of benefit in others.

In the *Methodist Hymnal* and in the *Book of Worship for Church and Home* there are two forms for the administration of the Lord's Supper—(1) a long order and (2) a brief one. General instruction is offered here upon the brief order. Later on in this chapter suggestions in greater detail are provided for those congregations accustomed to the more elaborate service.

1. In the briefer service having issued the invitation urging all who "truly and earnestly repent of your sins" to join in the service, the minister leads the communicants into a proper preparation for kneeling at the Lord's table by asking all present to join him in the prayer of general confession, seeing that all need the sense of spiritual cleansing essential to a true fellowship with the Lord.

Almighty God, Father of our Lord Jesus Christ, Maker of all things, Judge of all men; we acknowledge and bewail our manifold sins and wickedness, which we from time to time most grievously have committed, by thought, word, and deed, against thy divine majesty, provoking most justly thy wrath and indignation against us. We do earnestly repent, and are heartily sorry for these our misdoings; the remembrance of them is grievous unto us. Have mercy upon us, have mercy upon us, most merciful Father; for thy Son our Lord Jesus Christ's sake, forgive us all that is past; and grant that we may ever hereafter serve and please thee in newness of life, to the honor and glory of thy name; through Jesus Christ our Lord. Amen.

If one finds himself leader of a congregation not accustomed to share with the minister in repeating these parts of ritual, probably his greatest service to that people will come as he so plans the worship from time to time as to teach them its proper use. They may never have realized the need in which they stand, never have possessed consciousness of the purifying of soul which comes through a meaningful confession. Because they were unaccustomed to group recital of these words, at first their sense of bungling may have discouraged participation and at the same time rendered them so self-conscious as to prevent any real spirit of confession or of worship. What more valuable contribution may a minister make to his people than simply to stop in the service, comment upon the meaning of the prayer, and by direct instruction and example lead them into a harmonious and satisfying performance of the rite!

When the people have offered their confession and have been directed to keep their eyes upon the ritual in prayerful spirit, let the minister, as representative of them all before God, make his petition to the Lord on their behalf:

Almighty God, our heavenly Father, who of thy great mercy hast promised forgiveness of sins to all them that with hearty repentance and true faith turn to thee; have mercy upon us; pardon and deliver us from all our sins; confirm and strengthen us in all goodness; and bring us to everlasting life; through Jesus Christ our Lord. Amen.

How natural at this point comes the response of the people in thanksgiving, once the minister has explained: "It is very meet, right, and our bounden duty, that we should at all times and in all places give thanks unto thee, O Lord, holy Father, almighty, everlasting God."

Therefore with angels and archangels, and with all the company of heaven, we laud and magnify thy glorious name, evermore praising thee, and saying: Holy, holy, holy, Lord God

83

of hosts, heaven and earth are full of thy glory. Glory be to thee, O Lord most high! Amen.

The more sincere and searching the confession they make and the greater their adoration of the Lord, the more truly men become aware of their own weakness and need. Consciousness that "I the chief of sinners am" is the condition of effective apostleship! And so, for himself and for those sharing with him in seeking the Lord, the minister speaks:

We do not presume to come to this thy table, O merciful Lord, trusting in our own righteousness, but in thy manifold and great mercies. We are not worthy so much as to gather up the crumbs under thy table. But thou art the same Lord whose property is always to have mercy. Grant us, therefore, gracious Lord, so to eat the flesh of thy Son Jesus Christ, and to drink his blood, that our sinful souls and bodies may be made clean by his death, and washed through his most precious blood, and that we evermore dwell in him, and he in us. Amen.

In but a moment they will be kneeling, receiving the elements of bread and wine which symbolize for them the act of God in Christ Jesus on their behalf, showing that "God so loved the world." With fitting words the minister, reading the prayer of consecration, talks with God concerning these elements, praying: "And grant that we . . . may be partakers of his most blessed body and blood."

Days before the celebration of the Lord's Supper let the minister and those who may be assisting him plan so thoroughly and become so familiar with every part of the ritual that there will be no halting or embarrassment. "There should be no distractions or innovations, and experiments should be avoided." All preparations for uncovering and covering the elements should be carefully rehearsed. "It is a time of sacramental silence in which the voice of God is heard. It is a time of self-examination, self-discipline and personal commitment," and no untoward word or movement should be allowed to distract the sacred commerce with the Eternal.

In Methodist custom, inherited through Mr. Wesley from the Church of England, the people come forward in a group (directed by ushers if the congregation is large) and, kneeling before the holy table, are served the bread and the wine. Retiring to their pews they are followed by another group, and still another, until all have been served. As the elements are distributed to each individual, the minister declares: "The body of our Lord Jesus Christ, which was given for *thee*, preserve *thy soul* and *body* unto everlasting life. Take and eat this in remembrance that Christ died for *thee*, and feed on him in *thy heart* by faith with thanksgiving." Similar and suitable words are uttered as the wine is handed to each communicant. "It is an impressive order and emphasizes the fact that the soul is alone with God. God speaks and acts in behalf of each communicant."

In many congregations the people are more or less restless. The minister must remember that in this, as in all public services, a *director* is most essential. The minister is the center of attention. (That should humble him and insist that everything he does actually directs and aids those who follow him.) The minister should be "in charge" of every part of the service.

If possible the minister should have such help in the administration of the elements that he may be able to remain standing in the pulpit throughout the service and so keep his eye on the congregation that he may direct their every act

85

and thought. If ever he becomes so absorbed in the actual administration of the elements as to forget the people, they probably will forget him and the service and begin talking with each other about other matters.

But where the minister himself must perform every part of the service, he should so order the several details as to be continually speaking directly to those at worship in the pews as well as those at the chancel. Therefore, when the minister has completed serving a special group at the chancel, if possible he should return to the pulpit and from the pulpit speak the prayer or exhortation or word of dismissal and of guidance for those in the pew.

The time of the service should be so planned that there may be opportunity not only for receiving the elements but also for meditation thereon. The bread and the wine are as the grace of God; and each individual's meditation there is as the faith of response without which no saving experiences are enjoyed by the worshipers. To that end let the people be encouraged to remain kneeling there while the minister, by stanza of hymn, passage of scripture, or word of prayer, directs their thoughts. And let those selections be so chosen and so addressed to the whole congregation as to maintain among those in their pews, as well as among those kneeling before the minister, a continuing experience of worship. Numerous familiar hymns and scripture passages lend themselves to such use:

> When I survey the wondrous cross
>   On which the Prince of Glory died,
> My richest gain I count but loss,
>   And pour contempt on all my pride.
> —*Methodist Hymnal*, 148

Spirit of faith, come down,
  Reveal the things of God:
And make to us the Godhead known,
  And witness with the blood.
'Tis Thine the blood to apply
  And give us eyes to see,
Who did for every sinner die,
  Hath surely died for me.
                    —*Methodist Hymnal*, 183

Come unto me, all ye that labour and are heavy laden, and I will give you rest. Take my yoke upon you, and learn of me; for I am meek and lowly in heart: and ye shall find rest unto your souls. For my yoke is easy, and my burden is light.
                    —Matt. 11:28-30

And he opened his mouth, and taught them, saying, Blessed are the poor in spirit: for theirs is the kingdom of heaven. Blessed are they that mourn; for they shall be comforted. . . . Blessed are the pure in heart: for they shall see God.
                    —Matt. 5:2-4, 8

In similar fashion a group may be dismissed to their seats by means of brief prayers with the minister speaking to the Almighty concerning some need, experience, or virtue related clearly to those kneeling there—and likewise related to the ones in their pews.

2. The following outline from a pamphlet prepared by Dr. Warner M. Hawkins and Dr. Oscar Thomas Olson is that of Order I, which is intended to be a complete order of morning worship. The service is a simple one, with all of its parts essential to its full meaning. Therefore, it is not wise to endeavor to abbreviate it by omitting certain portions. There are places, of course, where choices can be made: for example, in the service of instruction the

minister has the choice of using the Ten Commandments, the Lord's summary of the law, the Beatitudes, or the passage from Isaiah 53:1-10.

A careful reading of the rubrics or directives will assist both minister and congregation in making the service a high spiritual experience. Dr. Olson's outline endeavors to interpret this drama in terms of our evangelical understanding of the Sacrament of the Lord's Supper.

I

THE RECOGNITION AND PRAISE OF GOD

The Organ Prelude

The Processional Hymn, or *The Hymn of Praise I:* "Holy, Holy, Holy, Lord God Almighty." . . . Thus the service of worship opens with a hymn of recognition and awe of the Holy Lord God of the universe, before whom all creation bows.

The Call to Worship. Here are given those attributes of the Lord God—Spirit, Light, Power, and Love—to which man responds in reverent praise: "Glory be to God on high."

The Gloria Patri. This paean of praise to the Lord God is the climax in the opening act of recognition and praise.

The Collect for Cleansing. . . . Before God's holiness man becomes conscious of his own imperfection, and of his need for cleansing before he is worthy to offer love and praise to the Most High God.

The Lord's Prayer

II

THE SERVICE OF INSTRUCTION

The Ten Commandments, the Lord's Summary of the Law, or the *Beatitudes of the Lord Jesus.*

The Scripture Lessons should be thoughtfully selected and set to the spirit and mood of the service.

The Apostles' Creed. This great historic affirmation of faith should be lifted, as a flag is raised, symbolic of the heritage of our Christian faith.

88

The Silent Meditation

The Pastoral Prayer. The priestly intercession of the minister should lift the worshiping people to a spiritual unity.

The Anthem may be of the type that meditates upon the sacrificial aspect of the life of Jesus, such as Stainer's "God So Loved the World," from *The Crucifixion* [or one of the Hymns in the *Methodist Hymnal;* 408 or 415 could be used].

The Communion Meditation. Here a brief sermon should set forth in eight or ten minutes some aspect of the sacramental life.

III

FELLOWSHIP AND GIVING

The Hymn of Fellowship now unites the people in a closer act of participation with their fellows in the experience of the corporate life.

The Alms Offering is a sharing on the part of the worshiping people in an offering of love to help lift the burdens of those who are in need. . . . During the taking of this offering the Scripture sentences indicated should be read. . . . This offering is the indispensable conclusion of all that has gone before: for God's forgiveness and acceptance of us leads us to efforts for the good of our fellows.

The Choral Response is an act of praise and thanksgiving sung by the choir and worshiping people as the minister places the offering upon the Lord's Table.

The Ascription of Praise should be said by the minister after he has placed the offering upon the Lord's Table.

IV

THE CONSECRATION OF THE ELEMENTS

The Invitation to Commune. . . . The mood of the service has now changed, and while the corporate element is present the appeal is to the individual heart and conscience. Here the individual soul of man is called into the presence of the God and Father of Jesus Christ.

The General Confession follows. . . . The minister leads in a confession of sin and a prayer for forgiveness.

The Prayer for Absolution is given by the minister in behalf of the people. The phraseology of this prayer . . . makes its efficacy dependent upon the inward attitude and motive of the worshiper. It should lead to a humbling experience by its very strength of ethical sternness.

The Comfortable Words bring the assurance of the teaching of the gospel to the soul that is sensitive of its own unworthiness to stand in the presence of the living God.

The Sursum Corda that follows is the upward lift of the heart that comes with the consciousness of sins forgiven.

The Preface definitely announces the obligation "that we should at all times and in all places give thanks" to God for the sacramental privileges of life.

The Sanctus that follows should always be sung as an act of thanksgiving in which the living worshipers are united with the eternal hosts. Here the sacrament unites the world of time with the world of the eternal.

The Prayer of Consecration now sets apart the Elements of bread and wine for consecrated use. The service now moves to the high moment that brings a sense of separateness to life. God draws near so that even the common becomes sacred. The symbols of time speak for the reality of the eternal.

The Prayer of Humble Access again recalls the privileges of all believers. Here is the identification by faith of the worshiper with his Lord.

V

THE COMMUNION

The Administration of the Sacrament sees the worshipers come to the Lord's Table and receive from the minister and those assisting him the Elements. . . . It is strongly felt by many that one minister and one only should read the Communion ritual and that those assisting be not heard, either in the ritual service or in dismissing the people. . . . Special effort should be made to prevent hurry or crowding. Ushers should be carefully instructed before the service so that it will not be necessary to intrude into the service any words of direction. . . . Let each

90

table be dismissed with a versicle such as "Let the peace of God be with you."

VI

THANKSGIVING

The Prayer of Oblation, the minister and people kneeling, is the final act of offering unto God "ourselves . . . a living sacrifice." The climax of Christian worship is the offering of life to the purpose of the God and Father of Jesus Christ.

The Gloria in Excelsis is the concluding act of praise. The people should stand and sing this hymn of praise. The service of Holy Communion opens on the note of praise. It runs the gamut of life's moods toward the Eternal and shares in the devotion, sacrifice, and consecration of Jesus Christ. The service closes with the hymn of praise that should always be sung by the entire worshiping congregation.

The Benediction should send the people out aware of the central place of Jesus Himself in the Christian faith, of the dependence of all Christians upon Him for their life with God and of their possession of God's life in the measure of their fellowship with one another.

The Organ Postlude [12]

SPECIAL COMMUNION SERVICES

1. Through the centuries—and apparently it is to continue so—the Sacrament of the Lord's Supper is best celebrated in the sanctuary, "where memories and sacred associations combine to minister to the spiritual life." If there are persons whose labor or circumstance is such that they are denied the fellowship of the morning service but are present at the evening service, then a second distribution of the elements may be provided at that time even though it may not

[12] From *The Communion Service with Music,* copyright 1938 by The Methodist Book Concern. Used by permission of The Methodist Publishing House.

seem proper to repeat the ritual leading up to the actual distribution of the elements. Such could be done conveniently and impressively in those congregations today in which an altar service is arranged for all who desire to kneel and pray for a season before formal opening of the service. The minister might indicate a section of the chancel to be used by those not present in the morning, and, while others are sending up their prayers to the Almighty, these could be served—quietly and effectively—the elements of the Holy Communion.

Still others may not be able to come to the sanctuary at any hour on Sunday. Justin Martyr tells us that during the second century, after those present had been served, the deacons took a portion of the sacred food to those who were not able to attend. Dr. Kerr, cited above, writes:

> In that day there were slaves who were not masters of their own time. Today there are multitudes of men and women who do not command their own time. There are servants in homes, men and women on night shifts, chauffeurs and workmen, doctors and nurses, who labor while others rest but who desire the strength and comfort which the Sacrament affords.[18]

All these the minister may serve, greatly to their soul's delight.

2. For those who are ill individual Communion sets suited to such private use are available today. Some saint may not have been able to leave home for months or years. Let the minister prepare himself especially for serving the Communion in such a circumstance. The room may not be so lighted as to make reading easy; no instrument may be

[18] *The Christian Sacraments* (Westminster Press, 1944), p. 110. Used by permission.

available for music, or there may be no one to provide the music. Let the minister memorize familiar passages of scripture, peculiarly adapted to such lonely, and often discouraged, persons. Fix in mind and learn to sing, without aid of instrument or other persons, hymns which have come out of triumphant experience and are able to induce the same sort of experience in that quiet service. And when scripture has been repeated and hymns sung and prayers of thanksgiving and petition have been offered, with the least of ritual let the emblems of the Lord's Supper be administered to the one abiding there. And even if the minister has never experienced it before, he will find it true:

> Ah! there on eagle wings we soar,
>   Where sin and sense molest no more;
> For heaven comes down our souls to greet,
>   And glory crowns the mercy-seat.

There should be no hurry about the service. Normal visitation should characterize the visit. But once the specific administration of the Communion has begun, dignity and order should prevail. When the celebration is concluded, the minister should depart at once, "allowing the ordinance to give its own message." Such is equally proper in hospital and in home.

5.

Baptism

But Peter, standing up with the eleven, lifted up his voice, and said unto them, Ye men of Judaea, and all ye that dwell at Jerusalem, be this known unto you . . . this is that which was spoken by the prophet Joel; and it shall come to pass in the last days, saith God, I will pour out of my Spirit upon all flesh. . . . Therefore let all the house of Israel know assuredly, that God hath made that same Jesus, whom ye have crucified, both Lord and Christ. Now when they heard this, they were pricked in their heart, and said unto Peter and to the rest of the apostles, Men and brethren, what shall we do? Then Peter said unto them, Repent, and be baptized every one of you in the name of Jesus Christ for the remission of sins, and ye shall receive the gift of the Holy Ghost. For the promise is unto you, and to your children, and to all that are afar off, even as many as the Lord our God shall call.

WHEN WE open the New Testament, we are face to face with the practice of baptism. Neither in the account cited above nor in any other in the New Testament is specific explanation given as to why *this* ceremony, rather than some different one, was being used. Apparently baptism was familiar to all those versed in Hebrew history and custom. The prophets had spoken of the Holy Spirit as being poured out upon the people; priests employed innumerable washings to fit men for participation in their worship services. When Jesus came to John in the wilderness, where many were undergoing this ceremony, John declared: "I indeed baptize you with water unto repentance: but he that cometh after me . . . shall baptize you with the Holy Ghost."

Just as repentance had been an experience of the Hebrew religion from its earliest days, but had assumed larger meaning with the development of the prophetic conception of religion, and had come to its climax in John the Baptist and Jesus, so also baptism—in the form of cleansings—ages old in application among both Jews and other peoples, when employed in the Christian religion became greatly different in content from its earlier uses. The first employment of circumcision appears to have been for purely physical advantage, but long before the days of the New Testament that ceremony had come to be treasured as of deeply spiritual significance. For every devout Jew it was a reminder of God's covenant with Abraham and his seed, and its observance was occasion for the deepening of that loyalty to God and to his purpose in the race.

As Jesus brought to completion the ideal of the prophets —that the kingdom "is within you"—men began to realize that Jehovah is the Father not only of Jews but of all men. The Master's expression of that truth is in his invitation: "If any man thirst, let him come unto me, and drink." God is ready, then, to enter into covenant with Jew and Gentile alike, as is set forth so clearly in the Epistle to the Ephesians —the same letter which speaks of "the church, which is his body." Therefore just as God's promises were seen as worldwide, including indeed but not limited to "Abraham and his seed," the mark and seal of that covenant with Abraham ceased to be fitted as an entry into the new and larger Christian fellowship. God the creator was the same, but the meaning of religion had come to be understood in completeness as never before, and those who might share in it were now seen to be the whole of mankind! It was not that circumcision was false and that baptism was true; it was that the conception of religion now swept far beyond that of people as a race in the eyes of God, just as in turn prophet and Messiah fulfilled the ideal of Jehovah for his children.

In the same manner in which circumcision had begun as a means of physical health and in later centuries had come to be associated with the most precious spiritual relationship between the race and the Almighty, so the cleansings—common in Jewish usage—developed in moral significance until when the forerunner of the Saviour was calling men, "Repent ye: for the kingdom of heaven is at hand;" "then went out to him Jerusalem, and all Judaea, and all the region round about Jordan, and were baptized of him in Jordan, confessing their sins."

This passing over of Hebrew lustrations into Christian baptism came with the development of the Hebrew religion into the Christian religion. It was not that the God of the Hebrews was different from him called Father by the Lord Jesus; rather was it that the prophets and Jesus had come to see in this Hebrew God the nature which was to be manifested in Jesus on the cross. Many customs which had served as "schoolmasters" for the race, in the "fulness of the time" bodied forth the inner, spiritual content of this religion of Jehovah.

One of the chief services of the Hebrew prophets was their intepretation of the ideals enshrined in the observances of Israel. Out of their prophetic insight they penetrated past the mere rite to the spiritual truth which was symbolized.

96

One of the most notable examples of this prophetic contribution is found in Ezekiel 36:25-26, "Then will I sprinkle clean water upon you, and ye shall be clean: from all your filthiness, and from all your idols, will I cleanse you. A new heart also will I give you, and a new spirit will I put within you: and I will take away the stony heart out of your flesh, and I will give you an heart of flesh." In such a way baptism came to be the symbol of the forgiveness of sins and the new life in Christ Jesus. This spiritualizing of religious rites occupied centuries.

PROSELYTE BAPTISM

One of the very familiar uses of baptism in its more strictly Jewish environment was what is called "proselyte baptism." Even before the coming of Jesus the higher ethical appeals of the Jewish religion were recognized by persons of other races, and many of them sought fellowship in this monotheism of Israel, with its emphasis upon the inner life, its moral ideal, and its holy God. They were called "proselytes," which is the Greek word for the Hebrew "resident aliens," or, as we would say, "newcomer." They were admitted into the Jewish religious fellowship through a ceremony of initiation which included circumcision, baptism, and sacrifice. With acceptance of the universal nature of religion taught by Jesus, of course Gentiles were no longer under necessity of becoming "Jews"; and as the "sacrifice of a broken and a contrite heart" gained in its appeal over the ceremonies of the temple, circumcision and sacrifice were gradually dropped, and the newcomer to the Christian group was received into its fellowship by baptism.

97

THE BAPTISM OF JOHN THE BAPTIST

In the first century a use of baptism even more meaningful to early Christians than proselyte baptism was that of John the Baptist. John is spoken of as the last of the great prophets. Added to all the moral idealism of his predecessors was his declaration that the day of the Messiah *has come*. This gave his call to repentance its urgency, and so his demand for moral purification was more imperative than had been that of any former prophet. This need for purification is what gave to the ceremony he employed such emphasis as led him to be called "John, the baptizer."

Although the Christian use of baptism, like that of John, continued to require as conditions repentance and faith, yet the distinctive meaning of that ceremony in the early church was *initiation* into membership in the group. This idea of initiation was not prominent in John's baptism. Those who came to him were not seeking to become members of a new community. His ceremony was to them a "sign and seal" of a moral and spiritual change. Thus John gave to this almost universal rite of baptism a depth of meaning hitherto unknown. He spiritualized it. It was an observance in which the participant registered his faith in God, gave witness to a spiritual quickening, and, through his repentance and confession, received a further blessing.

This ethical significance of John's baptism may be seen in his demands upon the penitents who flocked into his services. They were Jews. A spiritual revival was purifying their ideals and quickening their desires. Because they were convicted of laxness in obedience to the moral law, they came making open and public confession of their sins. Long had they looked forward to the coming of the messianic kingdom; they believed it now to be at hand. How appropriately, how vividly this moral and spiritual cleansing was symbolized by baptism!

In this ceremony of John the prominent idea was neither the change from one group into another group nor the conception later dominant in the Christian Church, that baptism washes away the guilt of sin; rather was it the great moral change which he demanded of Jews if they would enter into the Kingdom! This meaning cannot be missed. Looking out upon the multitudes who attended his meetings and asked to be baptized, John exhorted: "O generation of vipers, who hath warned you to flee from the wrath to come? Bring forth therefore fruits meet for repentance."

Thus, though repentance be the ground of entering the Kingdom, John seems to have realized the fitness of such an outward ceremony as baptism as a public mark of that inner change which had been made in the souls of the penitent ones. And yet, mindful of the coming Messiah whose way was being prepared by this his forerunner, John did not consider his baptism the end of that which was in store for all who followed his words. "I indeed baptize you with water unto repentance: but he that cometh after me is mightier than I, whose shoes I am not worthy to bear: he shall baptize you with the Holy Ghost, and with fire."

Jesus took up this use of baptism and gave it the significance which John had indicated: "For John truly baptized with water; but ye shall be baptized with the Holy Ghost not many days hence." "As the baptism of the proselyte was part of the ceremony of dedication by which a Gentile was incorporated into Israel, so John's baptism is an act of re-dedication by which Israelites, who through sin have lost their right to the name, may be incorporated afresh into the true Israel." [1]

CHRISTIAN BAPTISM

The basis of membership in the Jewish Church through the centuries had been birth, and the seal of the covenant between Israel and Jehovah had been circumcision, with preparation for many of its services made through cleansings by water. These cleansings came ultimately to be called baptism. In later centuries when, with decline of the national Israel, the moral appeals of monotheism and the high ethical standards championed by that people began to draw into its worship many persons from other races, proselyte baptism became prominent as means for their admission. Nothing is said in the Old Testament about this proselyte baptism "for the reason that it was not until later Judaism that proselytizing became common." The distinctive function of proselyte baptism was the making a Gentile a Jew.

But now that the kingdom of heaven was at hand, and through repentance and baptism at the hands of John men had signified their loyalty to it, Jesus came, standing for that fulfillment of Jewish history, ideals, and prophecy, and offering the baptism of the Holy Spirit. Into this new kingdom men were now invited to come; and they were invited not only to enjoy its salvation themselves but to become members of that fellowship which, after the days of the Master upon earth, would assume responsibility for promoting the work begun by their Lord: "the church, which is his body." This *joining* the Church, then, became that which above all else was signified by baptism. Christian bap-

[1] Hugh Thomson Kerr, *The Christian Sacraments* (Westminster Press, 1944), p. 44. Used by permission.

tism did not drop the requirement of repentance; it did not leave behind the "cleansing" of the Holy Spirit; but it gathered these up into the act of becoming a member in this universal Church of Jesus Christ. It may not be described in so many words, but initiation into the membership of the church is the characteristic use of baptism in all present-day churches. However genuinely religious persons may be, since the days of the New Testament they do not become members of the church without being baptized; and only in cases of rare exception are persons baptized when they are not joining the church. Exceptions come, of course, in small groups such as the Friends; and sometimes adults who are not joining the church do, for some greatly urgent reason, receive Christian baptism. Still, such exceptions do not set aside initiation into church membership as the distinctive use of baptism.

Too often in the Christian group today we do not make enough of this idea of *joining* the Church. "If we could recover something of the radiancy of early Christianity, baptism might become to us the sign and seal of the joy of the Lord and the peace of his salvation." [2] Next in importance to becoming by repentance and faith "a new creature in Christ Jesus" in his inner soul is the individual's openly becoming one of Christ's followers on earth. By that act, as our seventeenth Article of Religion indicates, "Christians are distinguished from others that are not baptized." The person publicly professes his faith in the Lord Jesus and claims the blessing of the Almighty in his inner life. His greatest joy henceforth will be found not in being ministered unto but in serving the Lord and his fellows. He is *joining* the Church; he is becoming a member of this body through

[2] *Ibid.*, p. 49.

101

which the kingdom of God is to become a reality among men. In its fellowship he may be increased in faith, confirmed in hope, and made perfect in love; through his loyalty to this body and to the keeping of God's holy will and commandments he may contribute his share to the edification of believers and the conversion of the world. In the days of the early Church this was a fellowship never before known. "There is neither Jew nor Greek, there is neither bond nor free, there is neither male nor female: for ye are all one in Christ Jesus." This was what was new in Christian baptism!

RISE OF DOCTRINE OF BAPTISMAL REGENERATION

Methodism had its rise in England, but its largest numbers have been gained in America. Jesus was a Jew, born in Palestine, yet the Church which bears his name made its early great development in the Roman Empire. As this Jewish-born Church became distinctively "Christian," proportionately fewer and fewer Jews were to be found within its membership, until within one hundred years after the last apostle the Church was all but exclusively Gentile.

Modification in ceremony and doctrine during the first three hundred years is just as evident as was that in membership and ministry. Certainly baptism did not originate in the mystery religions of Gentile bodies; yet, as the ministry and members of the Church were increasingly Gentile rather than Jew, the honest interpretation made of the means of salvation was noticeably Gentile. To find example of this modification, even in the first generation of the Church, one need go no further than to Peter and Paul. How much more of the "fatherly" conception of God, the divine image in man, the universal nature of the religion, the equality of the races before the Almighty, are to be found in the Greek-trained Paul than in Peter, the more characteristically Jewish apostle! And although we today deplore the Gentile development of Christian teaching and sacrament—moving away from the truly New Testament Christian value of repentance and faith—we cannot fail to recognize its source in the host of Gentile converts. However genuinely they were converted from their pagan religions to the Christian faith of their adoption, it would have been strange indeed had they not interpreted these new truths out of the background of their inheritance.

Christian theology was wrought out and shaped, not in the Hebrew, but in the Gentile world. Its great thinkers and teachers, after the first century, were Greeks and Greek-speaking men. So that while the rites of these pre-Christian Mysteries cannot be brought into any connection with the origin of the Christian sacraments, they had a most vital, and it may be said, permanent, influence on all the accepted Christian sacraments. The elaboration of the ritual, the demand for previous fastings, the celebration of the rites at certain seasons, especially at Easter, the tendency to secrecy, and the excluding of outsiders, and even the use of such terms as "the enlightened," and "the sealed," all reveal how potent the rites of the Greek mysteries had proved themselves in their effect on the Christian mind.[3]

The coming into the Church of this overwhelming number of people, with their sense of value and habits of thought being that of the Gentile pagan world, was the occasion for that development in doctrine and in ceremony which changed the distinctively New Testament ideas and practices into those which through the centuries have characterized the Roman Catholic Church. In doctrine this new

[3] W. M. Clow, *The Church and the Sacraments*, pp. 65-66. Used by permission of publisher, James Clarke & Co., Ltd.

emphasis showed itself in the idea of original sin, that man comes into the world with an inherently corrupt nature; in sacrament it is the conception of baptismal regeneration. Given a nature that is corrupt, a mind that is helpless to understand, and a will unable to act, a ceremony that is capable of washing away this guilt is normal. Speaking specifically of baptism, but in logic equally meaningful in relation to original sin, Dean Arthur Stanley writes:

No doctrine has ever arisen in the Church more entirely contrary to the plainest teaching of its original documents. In the Old Testament, especially in the Psalms,—where the requisites of moral life are enumerated as alone necessary to propitiate the Divine favor,—it is needless to say that Baptism is never mentioned. In the New Testament the highest blessings are pronounced on those who, whether children or adults, had never been baptized.[4]

The doctrines of original sin and baptismal regeneration go naturally together, and the two had their beginning, in any real emphasis in the Christian Church, during the days between the Twelve and Augustine. True it is that both teachings are supported today by quotation from Paul, but those doctrines today are in relation to Paul only in the same way in which in earlier centuries circumcision and baptism passed from one stage into another, becoming in the end very different indeed from what they were earlier.

To say that early Christian teaching and custom changed into characteristically Catholic conception between A.D. 100 and 400, while the Church was being emptied of Jews and filled with Gentiles, is not to assume that Gentiles alone brought this significant development. Much of similar

[4] Arthur P. Stanley, *Christian Institutions*, pp. 17-18.

change may be found to have taken place in those religious bodies which remained Jewish in membership. During this period of three or four hundred years corresponding change was being made in the life within that Mediterranean world.

We find example of this fact of modification in political theory during the past three hundred years in our modern world. In the seventeenth century there was hardly a nation in the world not ruled by a king; in the twentieth century there is to be found no single monarch who in reality governs his people. Three centuries ago persons in the state were characteristically subjects; in society they were servants. Today the goal attained by millions is that of citizenship—and those who do not possess that status yet are striving with vigor for it!

The development from A.D. 100–400—the period in which the early Christian Church became the Catholic Church—was in exactly the opposite direction from that in which our modern world has been moving. The Roman Republic was becoming the Roman Empire. Instead of a nation ruled by senate and forum, the empire came to possess a ruler who both claimed and exercised absolute power over his people. And—in every age—a people who are unable to control themselves politically and must depend upon someone to rule over them have found that in the matter of salvation the individual assumes that he is himself unable to exercise saving faith and so must depend upon the priest and the church to do that for him. It was within a society holding that conception of God and man and the state that there developed a Church whose characteristic teachings were original sin and baptismal regeneration. And that kind of state and Church continued throughout the Middle Ages. Right down to the days when Martin Luther insisted upon a straightforward interpretation and application of the New Testament, this medieval teaching continued, classifying men in society as masters and servants, in politics as sovereign and subject, in religion as priest and people.

How different from the New Testament conception: "Believe on the Lord Jesus Christ, and thou shalt be saved"! What another means from that voiced in the Scriptures: "If we will confess our sins, he is faithful and just to forgive us our sins, and to cleanse us from all unrighteousness"! Not until the coming of Protestantism was insistence made upon a restoration of this prophetic, this New Testament, teaching concerning God and man and salvation; and although the change from the Middle Ages idea has been a slow one—both in state and in church—since Martin Luther proposed that we follow the Bible as our guide to salvation, the doctrines of original sin and baptismal regeneration have been on the decline. In the world today wherever the state holds a heavy hand upon the people, the Church continues to assert itself as the only means of salvation; but where the conception of man is thoroughly democratic, the state has tended to become the servant of the people, and the Church a "means" rather than the source of salvation. Jesus Christ is the *source;* the Church is the *means* of bringing men into saving contact with this source of salvation. Within any large body of people—where freedom of thought and worship are present—of course will be found men of different understanding. So that today in a great democratic country like America there are those who cling to the Catholic inheritance of original sin and baptismal regeneration; but as democracy increases, in both state and church, the worth of the individual advances, and the "whosoever will" teaching of Jesus is on the march!

6.

The Baptism of Infants

"TO ABRAHAM and his seed," "he and all his" (the jailor), "the house and family of God," and similar phrases appear with such frequency in religious literature as to seem normal expressions of the relation of children to the Church. Not only so but as far back as authentic accounts bear record, religious bodies have employed some formal ceremony by which they have endeavored to guarantee proper relation of their children to the divinity which the parents worshiped. The understanding of God maintained by a people and the customs of their inheritance give form to such a ceremony, so that in the measure in which Christians think differently from other religious groups concerning the Almighty, the ceremonies for their children are different in meaning from others. But God has made of one blood all the races of men, and historians know of no large body of people who, having sought to worship the Eternal, have not by some formal ceremony endeavored to bring their children into his favor.

The more "primitive" a religion is found to be, the more clearly physical its ceremony is. Among the early Hebrews the ceremonies employed to present their little ones to Jehovah were primarily of the nature of physical cleansing. But as their religion became increasingly spiritual, so also did its ceremonies for their children. Up from positive bodily cleansing, on the ground of physical well-being, the custom moved into the realm of religion and, in most instances, assumed not literal but symbolic cleansing. We are very sure that when Hannah and Elkanah presented Samuel to the Lord, and when Joseph and Mary brought the child Jesus to the Temple, there was in their hearts a parental religious intelligence both in harmony with the customs of their day and pleasing to the God to whom they committed their little ones. That which earnest parents do today in having their children baptized has continuity with the devout in all ages and among all the religions of mankind.

RELATION OF CHILDREN TO THE CHURCH DURING NEW TESTAMENT DAYS

"Ye shall neither in this mountain, nor yet at Jerusalem, worship the Father. . . . The true worshippers shall worship the Father in spirit and in truth." This represents the ideal attitude of men toward God as announced by the Master. But men are body as well as soul; they approach that ideal out of their inheritance and in their own halting manner. The race in which Jesus was born had conceived of themselves as the specifically chosen people of the Almighty, and so the mere matter of blood inheritance was in their sight essential to membership in the family of God. Therefore it had been their thought that birth into the Jewish race was condition to salvation. And so, although in the days of the New Testament this spiritual ideal had been greatly purified, the age-old, normal concern of parents for their children was not relaxed even though the Christian conception of their relation to the Church had been made more real. We are certain there was much less of the idea of

108

physical cleansing and more of the symbol of spiritual
purification in the ceremony sought for Jesus by Joseph and
Mary than there had been centuries earlier when devout but
more primitive parents brought their children to the priest.
And although no positive mention of the baptism of an
infant is made in the New Testament, since no intimation
is given there that the Master taught that such bringing of
their little ones to the Lord was contrary to his view of religion, one cannot help believing that a custom so tenacious
in the thought of previous generations was not shortly set
aside. Instead, the very tender attitude which Jesus assumed
toward little children, and his using them as an illustration
of the ideal innocency in his religious teaching of adults,
strengthens belief that such an act as their early dedication
to the Lord was looked upon only with favor.

The New Testament tells us almost nothing of the experience of Jesus from early infancy until he was twelve
years old, and then his name drops out of attention until he
was about thirty years of age. Does this silence of the
sacred Book warrant conclusion that for ten years first,
and then for eighteen more, the child Jesus ceased to
be? When through the centuries of patriarch and prophet
accounts are abundant that devout Jewish parents dedicated
their children to God in ceremonies corresponding to our
baptism of infants, and then as tender and challenging as
was the service in which Mary and Joseph brought to the
Temple the "only begotten Son of God," do we believe
that because the pages of the New Testament thereafter do
not name some specific child as being thus consecrated to
God, children no longer were precious in the eyes of the
Almighty, and that devout parents so suddenly came to
condemn such earnest manifestation of concern for the

religious welfare of their offspring as had characterized all previous centuries of the Hebrews and of religions in all ages? And when the Fathers of the second century speak of the baptism of infants as an "apostolic" practice, do we say they were mistaken in their concern and ought not to have practiced baptism—even though we have in the record no single intimation of the Lord's instructing parents to drop off that custom? Such a conclusion would be no more warranted than to say that because the New Testament does not tell us what the boy Jesus was doing from the time of his appearance in the Temple at twelve up to the day when he appeared in the synagogue to declare: "This day is this scripture fulfilled in your ears," therefore Jesus was not alive during those years!

WHY THE NEW TESTAMENT IS SILENT UPON INFANT BAPTISM

The slight attention given to young children in the New Testament account is not disturbing, but instead is normal. "Go ye into all the world, and preach the gospel." To whom were they to *preach?* What mention is made of young children in the "revival" conducted by John the Baptist? Search through the sermon themes of the days of the Great Awakening in America, around 1750; how many times is Jonathan Edwards, or the Tennents, or George Whitefield recorded as having preached about infants? How much time in his revival campaigns did Dwight L. Moody, or Sam Jones, or Charles G. Finney, or William A. Sunday preach upon that theme? The New Testament is an account of the great spread of the Christian religion during the first century; the purpose was a wholesale propagation of Christian truth, aimed directly at convincing and converting

110

adults of all races and tribes. And how successful was that campaign!

Then when by the middle of the second century many communities were nominally Christian, and among those people the continued growth of the Church would depend primarily upon the coming in of the children of Christian parents, how natural that the Fathers are found talking about the baptism of infants—and also how natural that they should speak of it as an apostolic custom! In the great proportion of all Christian bodies since that time devout parents have felt under obligation and have found solemn delight in bringing their sons and daughters to the altars of the church and there dedicating them to the service of the Lord. Of course no parent can commit the will of the child to God, nor compel any son or daughter to serve the Lord; that is a matter of individual faith; but anxious fathers and mothers can at the altar of the church make earnest promise to God and to friends to live before their children as becomes the gospel, and so fulfill the scriptural injunction to train up a child in the way he should go. It seems strange indeed that such an act on the part of parents and church should be declared contrary to him who said, "Suffer the little children to come unto me, and forbid them not: for of such is the kingdom of God."

CHILDREN AND THE CHURCH IN THE MIDDLE AGES

Just as during the centuries of the modern world the Arminian conception of God and man replaced that held by Calvin and by the Church in the Middle Ages, exactly so but in the opposite direction, as the Church of the early days came to be made up of Gentiles rather than of Jews, the doctrine of original sin supplanted that "whosoever will"

111

teaching of Jesus, operating through what we call "justification by faith." That interpretation of child nature was made popular and binding by Augustine. In his earlier years he had doubted whether so harsh a doctrine could be held; but in full age, "God forbid," he said, "that I should deny that truth." And when they brought him the case of a child who had died without the possibility of being baptized, he bemoaned its fate but adjudged that infant forever lost. Such an understanding held sway in the Church as late as the time of George Whitefield and John Wesley. Whitefield argued that every man comes into the world totally depraved; he believed that Jesus Christ died not for all men but only for the elect. So great was his emphasis upon "by *grace* are ye saved" that he had no prominent attention for Paul's other statement in the same passage: "through *faith*." Upon that issue the early prominent founders of Methodism were unable to agree, and they became completely separate in their revival efforts. Calvinistic Methodism (promoted by Whitefield) today is a mere sect, whereas Arminian Methodism numbers its members in the millions.

BAPTISM A REMEDY FOR ORIGINAL SIN

For fifteen hundred years the water of baptism was called holy, and it was believed that the priest who administered the rite had supernatural power through its use to wash away the stains of sin and to absolve the soul from guilt. During the same period it was taught that by miracle the priest changes the bread of the Lord's Supper into the flesh of Jesus and the wine into his blood. During those centuries kings claimed to rule by divine right; the masses of men were born to serve and the few to rule. "Baptismal regeneration" was normal under that conception of God and man

112

and society, and it remained the teaching of the Church concerning its sacraments until once more men turned their eyes back upon the New Testament and its interpretation of the gospel. When that occurred, when Luther declared the supremacy of the Scriptures over tradition; when he asserted that individual repentance and faith, rather than the sacraments, are the grounds of salvation, then began to decline the idea of baptismal regeneration. Men began to see themselves as equal in the sight of God, and the day of master and slave, of kings and popes, was turned toward its sunset.

Changes in basic custom and doctrine come slowly; the form continues generations after the truth concerned has taken new meaning; so that down into the times of Wesley, of early American Methodism, and, though in diminishing force, even to this twentieth century, those conceptions have persisted. But given the solid New Testament teaching of justification by faith, both original sin and baptismal regeneration are on the decline. The first ritual for the baptism of infants in The Methodist Church opened by saying: "Dearly beloved, forasmuch as all men are conceived and born in sin"; the corresponding paragraph today reads: "Dearly beloved, forasmuch as all men are heirs of life eternal and subjects of the saving grace of the Holy Spirit." While Methodism was making that transition, the American people joined in the fight for their freedom, the Declaration of Independence was signed, the Constitution of the United States was adopted, and slavery was overthrown; and we stand today the most thoroughly democratic people on the earth. These changes all flow out of our conception of God, man, and society; and in theology the classic phrase for this conception is justification by faith.

113

METHODIST UNDERSTANDING OF THE BAPTISM OF INFANTS

Strange as it may seem to his successors today, Wesley's *Works* contain the following statement, representing the teaching of the church of his fathers:

As to the grounds of it: if infants are guilty of original sin, then they are proper subjects of baptism; seeing, in the ordinary way, they cannot be saved unless this be washed away by baptism. It has been already proved, that this original stain cleaves to every child of man; and that hereby they are children of wrath, and liable to eternal damnation. It is true, the Second Adam has found a remedy for the disease which came upon all by the offence of the first. But the benefit of this is to be received through the means which he hath appointed; through baptism in particular, which is the ordinary means he hath appointed for that purpose.

The more logical teaching of Methodism—consistent with its championing of the "free moral agency of man"— rests upon the conception of God and man involved in the "whosoever will" of Jesus. It goes back likewise to the prophets. While about him were men following the idea of inherited sin, Ezekiel (ch. 18) asks, in effect: Why do you say, "The fathers have eaten sour grapes, and the children's teeth are set on edge?" And then he explains, "As I live, saith the Lord God, ye shall not have occasion any more to use this proverb in Israel. Behold, all souls are mine. . . . The soul that sinneth, it shall die." The prophet then illustrates the truth he has declared. "If a father transgress my law, and die in his sins, he shall be lost. But if that father beget a son, who does not follow in his father's way, but does that which is right, that son shall not die because of his father's sins, but shall be saved." The teaching corollary to this truth is that if ever there is forgiveness, if ever "a new creature in Christ Jesus," it must come as set forth in Paul's letter to the Romans—through genuine repentance and faith of that same person, trusting in the grace of God! That is the ground of Methodism's teaching and use of the baptism of infants today.

The statistical blanks by which the Methodist preacher makes a report each year to the Annual Conference have columns for persons received into the church during the past twelve months: "by profession of faith," "by certificate," and so on. These blanks likewise have a column giving the number of infants baptized during the year, but this figure is never included in the totals for those who have been received into the church during the year. No, baptism of an infant does not admit that child into the membership of The Methodist Church.

Concerning the relation of baptism to the religious condition of the one receiving that rite, long ago Dr. Thomas O. Summers explained: "So far as can be seen, or as appears from Scripture, no moral change takes place in circumcision or baptism." And that is our teaching concerning the relation of baptism to the religious state of the adult as well as of the infant. That is our understanding of all sacraments, and for all persons receiving them. No physical ceremony can work a moral or spiritual change. Apart from the faith and resolve aroused in the person as a result of the service, the one receiving the rite remains as he was before it was performed. In the wedding ceremony, upon the same principle, we say: If the young man and the young woman while marching down the aisle do not have genuine love one for the other, there are no words intoned by the minister which are able to guarantee that as they go marching out, they are in deed and in truth husband and wife! Love may be "in-

115

duced"; it cannot be "compelled." And so with all ceremonies performed by the church in relation to religion. We believe sacraments are useful, and we believe Jesus approved them; we would not rob ourselves of their great benefits; but we believe they are really *means* of grace, that they do not *confer* grace. "Believe" and be baptized; "if we confess our sins, he is faithful and just to forgive us our sins." Methodism is firm in its conviction that apart from faith there is no salvation!

In reality, then, the great question concerning the baptism of infants is: How may children become religious? In answer to that question let us ask another: How do *adults* become religious? How may a bad man forty years of age become a good man? All these years that man has been facing daily the two ways of life—the good and the evil—and deliberately he has chosen the evil. In the life of that man the law that as you sow, so also shall you reap has been operative from day to day. Habit is cumulative, so that, granted that as he entered the experience of moral accountability, he was equally able to take the good or to choose the evil, as a result of these years of wrongdoing his powers are no longer thus balanced. Through the exercise of his "free moral agency" he has become hurtfully set in preference for that which is bad. So that if ever a sinner is brought to trust God, to delight in his fellowship, something must be done for the sinner which he cannot do for himself. Someone must help the transgressor to see that God does not desire to hurt him, but is seeking to forgive and restore him in heart and in life.

This thing which the sinner needs to have done, but which he cannot do for himself, seems to be what Paul had in mind when he wrote, "By grace are ye saved through

116

faith; and that not of yourselves: it is the gift of God." In another place it is said, "We love him, because he first loved us." Like Adam and Eve, every sinner is afraid of God and runs away from him. But whenever any Adam or Eve realizes that God loves rather than hates the sinner, then that one may respond "through faith" to the grace that is offered.

If it is thus in yielding to God's love that adults become Christian, how do children become Christian? Let one answer as before: By the grace of God children are saved through faith, exactly as are adults! The grace of God brings to consciousness in the heart of the child, as he matures, the fact that God loves him, and so encourages him to resolve not to follow in the way of evil but to walk in the paths of righteousness. The turning from sin to God by the adult is what we call conversion; it is the deliberate, purposeful commitment of the individual to God.

Now the child is in some respects different from the adult. Children, we believe, are born in innocency, not guilty of inherited sins; they are possessed of a capacity which at the opening of accountability enables them to enter upon the way of salvation or upon the way of sin, depending upon the choice to be made by the child. Certainly the adult considered above came into the world in such innocency; but when, as Mr. Wesley says, "the first faint ray of moral understanding dawned upon him," he chose the way of evil rather than the way of good. At that first opportunity of deciding between good and evil he had not already committed sin; there was no evil past *from* which he must turn away. Choosing the evil instead of the good, and continuing so to do for forty years, he was under necessity of turning away from sin. He became able to make so great a change because of his consciousness of the grace of God expressed in Jesus Christ. But if when for the first time he was faced with the alternatives of good and evil, that child had responded to the grace of God, had chosen to do righteousness rather than that which was bad, then we would say that by this choice the child as truly turned away from the *possibility* of evil, was just as truly *converted* as was the adult of forty years when he purposefully turned from sin to God. The conversion is in the turning to God, and the turning to God, whether as an adult or as a child, is in response to the love, the grace, of God.

THE TASK OF THE CHURCH

Now our concern as workers in the home and in the church school is how we may bring a child to exercise that act of saving faith back there at the first dawn of moral consciousness, rather than at some distant adult experience after years of rebellion against God have intervened.

Every normal child, we believe, comes into the world endowed with capacities necessary for happy and fruitful living. In physical person at birth the child is not in such control of his abilities as to exercise that co-ordination of mind and body which we exemplify in adulthood. But surely in germ the capacity is there when the child is born, and it waits only for those experiences which under proper direction and effort may come by normal development through the years.

So also we think of the young child as having a mind which under effective instruction and activity may come at the proper stage to grapple with the problems of mathematics, the beauties of literature, and the realities of the scientific and philosophical world. Endowments vary of

118

course in different individuals, and we realize fully that "education" in any worth-while realm can neither be imposed upon the developing child nor come as a free gift from anxious parents or teachers. Parents and teachers here on earth, as our heavenly Father, may surround the child all the days of his life by that willingness to help, signified by the term "grace"; but if ever that one becomes a "child of God" in any of these fine realms, it will be as an achievement of his own, a working out of his salvation, that response to this presence of grace, called by the apostle "faith." Thus there is God's part in one's salvation, always necessary and precedent; and equally there is man's part, always in response, always deliberate achieving, whether in the realm of body or mind or soul.

Though ultimately the responsibility rests upon the child, "through faith," we as older ones must never forget our part; God's endowment and grace, the nurture and admonition with which parents and friends may surround the child! Mr. Wesley had in mind that obligation of parents when he reasoned: If a child from birth should be reared under such circumstance that it never heard another person talk, that child would come to maturity uttering sounds but never arranging them into an articulate language. It is only as growing children have association with persons employing a spoken language that the children learn to express their ideas in intelligible words. And as it seems Mr. Wesley intended to say, it is only as the growing child, possessed of an ability to love God and his fellows, is surrounded by an environment—such environment always including not only men and women but *God* as primary—in which grace and love challenge faith, that that child can become a genuinely and consciously religious being.

119

One hundred years ago Dr. Stephen Olin said God intends the family to be a school of Christ, in which the child shall learn religion just as he learns a thousand other things: through the spirit and atmosphere of that association. Supplementing that most fundamental of all schools, the family, we today add the help of the church school, an institution but in its infancy when Dr. Olin uttered the above wise words.

We will remember, of course, that religion cannot be bestowed upon the child; we will not forget that truth for which Methodism was for so many years distinctive: the idea of the "free moral agency" in every man. Neither family nor church can guarantee that every child so nurtured will at the dawn of discretion, or even in later adulthood, exercise saving faith. Yet we cannot help being aware that our part is that of providing "grace."

We will not expect that the little one's act of faith be complete at first; nevertheless it may and should be "saving" since it is all that the child at that stage of development is capable of having. Moral understanding is itself a growing experience. "The becoming of a person is never finished." God requires of a person, at any given time, only that of which the individual is then capable.

When the bacon was passed at breakfast, a child about two and a half years old declared: "Thank you; you're welcome." Pleased as the parents might be at such words, an observer would reason that this statement indicated simply imitation rather than evidence of conscious courtesy. But one will not overlook the fact that imitation is based upon something of desire to repeat the words expressed.

The child had heard those words, they were a part of his environment, and they had been heard by him under such pleasing circumstances that he now chose to repeat them. These words would never have been uttered by the child—even be they simply imitation—had they not first been heard by that little one! Parents cannot be certain that by their being courteous before their little ones those children will grow up to be genuinely cultured souls, but every evidence we know convinces us that such environment is the most helpful circumstance possible for inducing in the child, as he grows, the spirit of real courtesy. So that should the child at ten or twelve years utter those same words, now separating the two phrases as is proper, parents have a right to believe that they are no longer imitation but an intended expression of an abiding sense within. This is but to affirm: "Train up a child in the way he should go: and when he is old, he will not depart from it." We know of no other way to help our children to become conscious of the grace of God than by living before them a life that "becometh the gospel," and thus to encourage them to respond to that grace *through faith*.

PURPOSE OF THE BAPTISM OF INFANTS

Such exactly is the purpose of infant baptism. We want to say to congregation and parents, here is a little one who is capable of becoming a great good man; likewise he may grow up filled with sin and wickedness. Which of these two he is to become will depend upon his own deliberate choice. But the primary influence in helping him to make that choice is the example, the instruction, the association, which that child is to have during the years in which he is becoming aware of the reality of good and the reality of evil.

Now the minister may teach this same truth in his earnest sermons from Sunday to Sunday. It should be held up from

121

time to time in the studies of the church school. But just as we employ the several means of grace—prayer, reading the Scriptures, public worship, the sacraments, each in its place more effective than any other—to teach some given truth, so we believe that by use of an objective ceremony like that of infant baptism, the possibility of influencing the tender mind of the growing child in favor of righteousness may be impressed upon congregation and parents more effectively than by any other agency.

What good can a few drops of water do, sprinkled on the head of an unconscious child? it is asked. In historic answer Methodism replies, it can work no immediate good in the heart of that little one; nor could an ocean of water add to or subtract from that one's religious state—nor indeed if applied to an adult! We assume that moral character cannot be either created or bestowed by ceremony. Salvation—to be like God, gracious, loving, forgiving, in our own souls—is by grace, through faith!

What good, then, can a few drops of water sprinkled on the head of a child do? Father and mother, standing at the altar of the church, love that little one better than they love their own lives. If to guarantee its happy future the giving of their lives were necessary, not one moment would either of them hesitate. Now the minister wants to say to them: The religious choices of this child as he grows to maturity will depend more largely upon your example, your instruction, than upon any other single influence. I want to help you here to realize that solemn fact. To that end I want you to make promise before this congregation that so far as in you lies, the Lord being your helper, you will seek to lead this child into the love of God and the service of the Lord Jesus Christ!

The vows of the wedding ritual do not create love of husband for wife, but experience teaches that such ceremony has helped husbands through the years of married life to remember to love and cherish the wives whom they have thus before God and the congregation made their own. Human society has never found other means equivalent to this one for maintaining happy family lives. So also with the ceremony of infant baptism. If that vow assumed by fathers and mothers at the altar of the church strengthens them during the years ahead in living before the child as they ought, then what incalculable benefit has been achieved on behalf of that child by the sacred act of baptism! Though Jesus Christ died for every child, not every child responds "through faith" to such grace. Many children it may be, dedicated by their parents in baptism, and observing fulfillment of those vows in Christian conduct and instruction, as they grow to maturity, may refuse to yield their lives to that ideal. But as God knew no other means quite so effective as the coming into the world in the person of Jesus Christ to teach men of God's grace, so also Methodists believe that in spite of the fact that children may exercise their free moral agency in refusal to follow the example of their parents, yet such vows and the quality of life encouraged thereby have no superior in the help that may be offered their little ones in becoming really Christian. Therefore, as our seventeenth Article of Religion declares, "the baptism of young children is to be retained in the church."

OCCASION FOR RENEWED INTEREST IN INFANT BAPTISM

There is no important place for a program of Christian nurture under the doctrine of original sin. As was indicated above, even in The Methodist Church for many years that doctrine was held concerning children. In his theory of prevenient grace Mr. Wesley in fact denied, although his terminology continued to be that of, inherited depravity. He made considerable advance in his conception of adults, insisting that every man has the ability to realize his sins and repent of them. But in the understanding of child life and in his doctrine of human nature he was little ahead of Luther or Calvin.

Such is not now true of Methodist leaders. Whereas once the church school was opposed by the denominations in America—and the Methodists gave to it no enthusiastic support for many years—now next to the pulpit the church school is recognized throughout Protestantism as the primary agency of the church. Magic, the sacerdotal, is rapidly passing; and religion is being looked upon as normal to experience. The modern understanding of the child denies the assumption of inherited guilt, of depravity, and works on the theory that as the physical and mental faculties grow, so religion may be developed—through conscious, meaningful choice—from infancy to old age. Recognition of this capacity for religious development gives to the child an entirely new interest in the eyes of the Church.

To those who believe in the doctrine of Christian nurture for children, there is no strong appeal in such arguments as were used even by Methodists for the support of infant baptism a hundred years ago. Children now are not baptized on the ground that they are under the "covenant." Further, so long as salvation was thought of as freedom from guilt, very great emphasis was placed upon confession; and such terms as justification, pardon, and merit were in the language of theology. The truth clothed in these terms is still precious to us, but today a more prominent element in religious terminology is "fellowship."

When does this fellowship of the child with God begin? When the child is old enough to confess his sins? When does fellowship between mother and babe begin? Long, long before the child is conscious of it. In fact, a normally developed family life so gradually, yet powerfully, shapes the life of the child that by the time he has reached maturity, in the usual case, his interests are in happy accord with those of the family. May it not be so in the child's relation to the heavenly Father? No infant simply "grows up Christian"; in order to be a Christian the infant, just as the adult, must deliberately commit his life to the Lord; he must be saved "by grace through faith."

This possibility of "growth in grace" for the young child, and the opportunity which parents and friends and the church have in so influencing him, is what is beneath the new interest in infant baptism. No more does the ceremony produce that fine condition than did the last supper of Jesus with his disciples create in them the love which they had for their Master. But the supper was an outward means of expressing that which was present in their hearts, of increasing it, and of continually reminding them of such as often as that meal might be observed. The presence of an infant at the altar of the church may have just that meaning in the minds of those who practice the baptism of infants!

7.

The Mode of Baptism

IN THE Christian Church today there are three modes of baptism: sprinkling, pouring, and immersion. Some small, though worthy, groups, such as the Friends, do not employ water baptism in any form; a few continue still the thousand-year-old practice of the Middle Ages, trine immersion. Trine immersion, so long the officially required mode, is based upon the idea that God is made up of three persons, Father, Son, and Holy Spirit. And so from the early centuries until modern times this mode was the law of the Church. The priest would say: "I baptize thee in the name of the Father (immersing the candidate in the water) and of the Son (a second time immersing the person), and of the Holy Spirit (immersing him a third time)." Fear that the use of this mode of applying water to the believer was helping to promote the heresy of polytheism—that there are three Gods, rather than *one*, and so to destroy the sense of unity in the Godhead—led the Church to relax its requirement; and so through the centuries of the modern world baptism has been performed by one application of the water.

During the long period in which there were "three baptisms" immersion was the legally recognized and applied form. Sprinkling or pouring was allowed in case of illness

126

or bodily infirmity, but up until approximately the days of Martin Luther there was little doubt in the Church that immersion was the really scriptural mode. In the same general period—the transition of the Middle Ages, into the modern age—in which trine immersion was changed into one immersion, sprinkling and pouring came to be recognized as equally valuable with other forms. That idea has prevailed for the past five hundred years, and now an even larger proportion of persons are admitted into the Christian Church by sprinkling than by immersion. The Greek Catholic Church continues immersion, the Roman uses sprinkling; Baptists, and Disciples of Christ, among our larger Protestant denominations, employ immersion only; while Presbyterians, Congregationalists, Lutherans, Protestant Episcopalians, and Methodists recognize both sprinkling and immersion, and leave to the individual to be baptized a choice as to the mode. So, as there are different nations in the political world, and as the followers of Jesus Christ are free to join this church or that, the ceremony by which their membership is signified may be performed in more than one way.

PHASES OF RELIGIOUS EXPERIENCE SYMBOLIZED BY BAPTISM

Whether set forth by sprinkling or pouring or by immersion, or even by trine immersion, there is one meaning in the ceremony common to all churches: in order to become a member in any of them, a believer in Jesus Christ must be baptized. In that respect baptism is different from salvation, even from the coming of the Holy Spirit into the lives of men. Apparently there was no act of baptism that day when Jesus said to Zacchaeus, "This day is salvation come to this house." And that fact is even clearer in the experience in which Jesus assured the penitent thief on the cross, "Today shalt thou be with me in paradise." The Ethiopian believed first and then was baptized; in the house of Cornelius as Peter preached, he beheld the Holy Spirit falling upon those who accepted his testimony; and Paul bore witness that in his services Gentiles had become possessed of the Holy Spirit while they were still outside any religious fold. But through the centuries, as men have obeyed the command of the Master and have asked to join the church, they have been baptized. Although few of our denominations today teach that baptism is essential to salvation, they are one in the requirement that church membership requires that one be baptized. And further, baptism is applied in no general way to persons who are not joining the church. If a revival meeting in a community results in the conversion of twenty persons, ten of whom unite with the church, and ten of whom do not, those ten who join the church will be baptized, whereas the other ten are not baptized. That is the common practice in all our churches, whatever mode of baptism may be exercised.

In addition to this experience of "joining the church," and in fact in most denominations as condition to it, there is the great reality of repentance. That was a note characteristic of the prophets, seven hundred years before the coming of the Messiah. John the Baptist urged those who came to him in the wilderness to repent; Peter stood up on the Day of Pentecost and called out to his hearers to repent and believe the gospel. We today do not know of any way of entering into the kingdom of God but by repentance.

Repentance, of course, is but a part of this "salvation process." First God surrounds men with his grace; in response to that grace men believe, repent; and then there comes the consoling, inspiring assurance of forgiveness. These are not two separate and unrelated experiences; although it may be said that one follows the other, in time, they are but two phases of the one saving relation to God.

For convenience and understanding and effectiveness in instruction, the minister may speak one Sunday on repentance; his subject the week following may be forgiveness. Baptism assumes both these experiences; it symbolizes or represents each one of them and so declares to all who observe, if you are to be saved and become a useful member of the church, you must both repent and be cleansed of your sins. What mode of the application of water may most effectively symbolize these experiences to him who is being baptized and to those who observe?

"Then Peter opened his mouth, and said, Of a truth I perceive that God is no respecter of persons: but in every nation he that feareth him, and worketh righteousness, is accepted with him." The setting, it will be recalled, was the house of Cornelius, where Jews and Gentiles had been called together in accordance with the direction given in visions to Peter and Cornelius. And "while Peter yet spake these words, the Holy Ghost fell on all them which heard the word. . . . Then answered Peter, Can any man forbid water, that these should not be baptized, which have received the Holy Ghost as well as we?"

Though it came to people whose customs were a little different from our own, and in figures other than are common to us, the reality is exactly the same as that which occurs upon a thousand occasions every year. What happened there was simply this: as Cornelius and his friends heard the message concerning the saving power of Christ, they accepted Christ and were filled at once with the Spirit of Christ. That is the experience which came to our fathers fifty years ago, when kneeling at the "mourners' bench" men repented of their sins, cried aloud to God for mercy, received the consciousness of forgiveness, and stood up to shout their praises to the Lord. Repentance, forgiveness, the witness of the Spirit, are all elements in every genuine conversion. And when such "saved" persons propose to take up their crosses and follow the Lord in the work of the church, they are baptized. What mode of baptism symbolizes effectively such a coming of the Spirit upon men?

At Pentecost when men "shouted" the praises of God, they were charged with being drunk; but Peter said, "This is that which was spoken by the prophet Joel . . . I will pour out of my Spirit upon all flesh." Today to symbolize this experience of genuine repentance, forgiveness, and the coming of the Spirit into their lives, some churches use sprinkling or pouring of water, some immerse the new believer in water; in that day, at Pentecost, when the apostles had been commanded to tarry in Jerusalem until the Holy Spirit should come upon them, and when the promise had been fulfilled before their eyes, Peter called it a "pouring" out of the Holy Spirit, and to symbolize that coming of the Spirit upon them three thousand were baptized. Of course neither they who were present at Pentecost nor we think of the Holy Spirit as a material substance, which could come by pouring, sprinkling, or immersion. But it is clear that Peter and the other apostles, that day at Pentecost, spoke of that baptism of the Holy Spirit of which the

130

prophets had spoken and which Jesus had promised, in the figure of pouring.

Most of our churches today would say, It matters not by what mode—pouring, sprinkling, or immersion—the coming of the Holy Spirit upon men is symbolized; our only interest in the use of water is that it may serve as an agency for impressing upon men's minds the reality of the Holy Spirit, and thus induce them to seek that cleansing, purifying, uplifting power in their personal lives.

And that of course is exactly, and all, that the immersionists seek in their use of baptism. They join with all others of us in the belief that cleansing from sin comes through repentance and faith on man's part, and the forgiving of sin on God's part; and this saving work must have been accomplished as condition to baptism. Baptism, for all of us, is a sign of that which has already come to be the experience of the believer.

"By grace are ye saved" is preached by all our denominations as the ground of salvation. And we are all agreed, too, that grace is made most clear and understandable to men by Jesus Christ, through his life, his teaching, his death, his burial, and his resurrection. That was precisely what Peter was preaching at Pentecost: "Ye men of Israel, hear these words; Jesus of Nazareth . . . ye by the hands of lawless men did crucify and slay . . . whom God raised up. . . . Being therefore by the right hand of God exalted, and having received of the Father the promise of the Holy Spirit, he hath poured forth this, which ye see and hear."

Describing the conversion of men to whom he was writing, the cleansing from their sins, and the experience of the Holy Spirit in their lives, Paul used the figure of the death, burial, and resurrection of Jesus, to which Peter

131

referred at Pentecost. As Jesus died, was buried, and then was raised from the dead, says Paul, ye were buried to your sins, ye were raised to new life, and now walk with him. How genuine is the experience of conversion to which Paul referred, and how apt and true and expressive is the figure which he used. Baptism by immersion certainly does symbolize most strikingly the physical death, burial, and resurrection of Jesus, and the spiritual death to sin and resurrection to a life of holiness in the experience of men.

But of course this death to sin, this burial of the "old man" and rising into new life of the man in Christ Jesus is exactly, not one whit more nor less, the experience in the mind of John the Baptist when he said, "Repent ye," and by Jesus when he urged, "Come unto me, all ye that labour and are heavy laden, and I will give you rest"; and by Peter, "Repent ye, and be baptized every one of you in the name of Jesus Christ unto the remission of your sins; and ye shall receive the gift of the Holy Spirit." Paul speaks of this in the figure of a burial and resurrection; Peter employs the image of pouring out of the Spirit. They were both right, and that which is symbolized by these two modes is the common experience of everyone who "feareth God and worketh righteousness." So that Baptist is right and that Methodist is right, and there is no genuine spiritual experience open to the Baptist in immersion that is not equally available and scriptural to the Methodist in sprinkling. Both modes were used in the New Testament times as both modes are used now, and we have no word in the New Testament that Jesus or Peter or Paul or any other in that day thought of one mode as being superior or inferior to the other mode. They had repented of their sins, God had graciously forgiven, they were walking in

132

the consciousness of the presence and power of the Holy Spirit, and by the use of water in joining the Church they gave testimony to this salvation through Jesus Christ. Concerning the mode or place of worship, "Neither in this mountain, nor in Jerusalem, shall ye worship," said Jesus, "but . . . in spirit and in truth." And when men had the spirit, then worship "in the mountain" was acceptable to God; and likewise those who rendered their devotions "in Jerusalem" were precious in his sight.

COMPARISON OF BAPTISM WITH LORD'S SUPPER
AS TO MODE

In the Lord's Supper no church today follows the minutiae of earlier centuries, even of that evening in the upper room; but no church thinks that such variation of the mode of administering the Lord's Supper affects its value for the sincere worshiper. Contention that immersion alone can be true baptism is usually based upon the fact that immersion was practiced in the days of the New Testament. Granted that immersion was used as baptism in the New Testament, this does not mean that no other mode was employed by the apostles, nor that in order to retain its effectiveness baptism must be always by immersion. Such an assumption throws baptism out of analogy with other Christian usages. Take, as example, the Lord's Supper. Surely the immersionists do not imagine that the usefulness of the Lord's Supper depends upon painfully conforming to the mode of its celebration there in the upper room.

The Lord's Supper was instituted at an evening meal, as part of a household feast which was itself the culminating act of an annual festival, from which it derived deep significance. It was held in a private gathering attended by men alone, who received the elements in a reclining posture. No one today seeks to reproduce any of these things in the celebration of the Lord's Supper. Even the use of unleavened bread is considered a matter of indifference by a large part of Christendom. This point of view is seen also in the substitution of grape juice for wine, and in the serving of this grape juice not in the common cup, as Jesus handed it from John to Peter and to the others of the Twelve, but in individual containers.

Jesus urged his followers to "do this in remembrance of me." And this is just as definite as his command to "baptize." But we have no word from him, or from any of his disciples, that in order for the Lord's Supper to be efficacious it must be held in the evening—the circumstance which gave it its name, Supper! There is no indication in the New Testament account that always it must be held in an upper room, by men reclining about a table, or that it must come always at the close of a regular meal. All these were present in that early observance of this sacrament, yet no one seems to have been conscious that any one or all of these together were essential to the benefit to be had in that ceremony.

Although there are today many different positions, taken by the several Christian bodies, concerning the proper time and mode of observing the Lord's Supper, we have no evidence that the actual benefit of that ceremony is dependent upon any one mode; neither do we have any evidence that it does accomplish for those who insist upon specific regulations what it does not accomplish for those groups who observe it according to a different mode.

The great fundamental experiences of cleansing, purification, commitment of life to the Lord are all present today, as in every age, in baptism. They are the permanent, the essential elements of the Christian life as represented in "joining the church." In every age there will be used those modes which make most meaningful in the minds of persons who are joining the church these living realities. Whatever mode may seem to achieve this purpose most perfectly will be employed by the church.

But just as in the days of the New Testament under varying circumstances different modes apparently were employed to represent these several truths, so in modern times there are groups which feel that one mode is more effective than another. Every one of these bodies retains as one and central the real spiritual cleansing, purification, commitment, and joining of the church. To fight or quarrel over the mode would seem—in the thought of Jesus—to be like quarreling over the mint and anise and cumin and overlooking the weightier matters—genuine repentance, trust in God, and commitment to his cause in the fellowship and work of the church. And for one group to denounce other bodies of those who believe in Jesus as Lord because those bodies do not use the same mode as that group, is to place the great realities of baptism upon the basis of the mint and cumin. Methodists endeavor to keep foremost the "weightier matters of the law," and to make such use of the mode as to keep the spirit central.

RELATION OF MODE OF BAPTISM TO DOCTRINE OF ORIGINAL SIN

A history of the modes of baptism shows that generally, through the centuries, when a church has believed in a rigid doctrine of original sin, it has been insistent upon immersion

135

as the only legitimate mode of baptism. As the Christian Church, with its Jewish inheritance, moved from Palestine out into the Roman Empire and recruited its members and preachers from among Gentile peoples, the rich experience of individual, personal repentance, assurance of forgiveness, and direct commitment to God passed out. The teaching triumphed that man has inherited the guilt of Adam's sin, is depraved and totally helpless; he can neither thank God nor do anything of value to him, and so the only thing that is really vital to his salvation is what God does for him. There grew up, therefore, the idea of a very rigid and specific method by which God brings salvation to men: a mode of baptism, legally prescribed, every detail in which must be exact and unvarying.

Emphasis upon that one specific mode lasted until the time of the Protestant Reformation, when once again attention came to be given to the New Testament experience of justification by faith. As this idea of salvation has grown, the churches are coming more and more to the freedom of the New Testament practice in the use or mode of baptism, because there is greater appreciation of the *experience* being signified; and so religion tends to become once more a fellowship with God rather than the result of the performance of a physical ceremony. Insistence upon some *one* mode of baptism is in reality to fall back upon the idea of "baptismal regeneration"; and as a matter of actual historical record, the teaching that immersion is the only use of water through which a genuine baptism may be had began and continued in and through the centuries in which the belief in justification by faith declined and there was held the idea that baptism washes away the guilt of sin.

This change of view is to be seen as early as the second

century, in the *Didachē* and in the writings of Justin Martyr and other postapostolic writers. In the mind of these incoming Gentiles appears an understanding of God, man, and the sacraments different from that of the New Testament. "There is a consciousness of the mode as such, and a sensitiveness to the minutiae of its performance. The New Testament is apparently unconcerned for the externals of the rite." It "refers incidentally to the fact that the element with which the ceremony is performed is water, and never introduces a hint that would deflect attention from the spiritual and social significance which the rite denotes." How different was Augustine's teaching of the place of baptism from Luther's teaching!

During this same thousand-year period the doctrine of original sin, the idea of the helplessness of the individual, the all but complete absence of the teaching of justification by faith, and the emphasis on its counterpart—baptism regeneration—constituted the thought and practice of the Church. But as society tended to become stabilized and the demand for the exercise of individual, saving faith increased, the earlier inherited prophetic and New Testament conception of justification by faith, and of baptism as a *symbol* of spiritual cleansing, tended to come back into appreciation. Along with this shift away from baptismal regeneration came a shift from the absolutist emphasis upon immersion, the making prominent once again of baptism as a symbol; and so sprinkling or pouring, as well as immersion, came to be seen as a visible sign of an invisible grace.

It is true that the Roman Catholic Church uses sprinkling, while continuing the idea of baptismal regeneration; but it is true also that the Roman Catholic Church of the late Middle Ages greatly modified its teaching upon the doctrine of original sin. It is true also that while he was writing out one of the most vigorous statements upon original sin, John Calvin prepared a ritual for use among his congregations allowing sprinkling, pouring, or immersion in baptism. But as centuries have passed, those denominations of Calvinistic background which have continued Calvin's belief that the mode of baptism is not essential have gradually given up his belief in the doctrine of inherited sin and depravity.

On the other hand, some of those denominations which insist upon "believers' baptism" hold to immersion. But it should never be overlooked that although "believers' baptism" groups require conversion before being baptized—and so in that way deny baptismal regeneration—yet they tell us that since Jesus commands baptism, all who disobey that command in refusing to be baptized by immersion will be lost. In reality, then, for such groups baptism is essential to salvation!

As the harsh doctrine of inherited sin has been softened by the Arminian idea that God loves all men, not just the elect, generally the churches teaching this New Testament emphasis of Jesus have shifted from the exclusive use of immersion to a recognition that the Christian experience of repentance, forgiveness, and joining the church may be represented as well by pouring or sprinkling. This change from immersion to sprinkling came first of all in England and in Germany, where the Protestant opposition to the doctrines of transubstantiation in the Lord's Supper and regeneration in baptism was greatest, and where justification by faith was preached with greatest confidence. Concerning this shift, the classic statement, *The History of Infant Baptism*, written by Wall generations ago, explains:

The offices or liturgies for public baptism in the Church of England did all along, so far as I can learn, enjoy dipping, without any mention of pouring or sprinkling.

In the Common Prayer Book, printed in 1549, the second of King Edward VIth, the order stands thus: "shall dip it in the water thrice." But this order adds: "and if the child be weak it shall suffice to pour water upon it, saying the aforesaid words." Afterward, the books do leave out the word *thrice:* and say, shall dip it in the water, so it be discreetly.

Upon review of the Common Prayer Book, at the restoration, the Church of England did not think fit (however prevalent the custom of sprinkling was) to forego their maxim; that it is most fitting to dip children that are well able to bear it. But they leave it wholly to the judgment of the godfathers and those that bring the child, whether the child may well endure dipping, or not; as they are indeed the most proper judges of that. So the priest is now ordered, "If the godfathers do certify him that the child may well endure it, to dip it in the water discreetly and warily. But if they certify that the child is weak, it shall suffice to pour water upon it." The difference is only this: by the rubric as it stood before, the priest was to dip, unless there were an averment or allegation of weakness. Now he is not to dip, unless there be an averment or certifying of strength sufficient to endure it.[1]

NO NEW TESTAMENT LAW AS TO MODE OF BAPTISM

When one sums up all the accounts of baptism, as recorded in the New Testament, there does not seem to be any specific rule as to the mode to be used; apparently different modes were employed by the apostles, without any thought that such variation was improper. "In John's mind and the people's, in Jesus' mind and the apostles', and in the thought of the early Church, the important thing was baptism itself" —the experience of belief in Jesus Christ as Messiah, of sorrow for sin, of consciousnes that sins had been forgiven,

[1] William Wall, *History of Infant Baptism,* I, 579, 583.

that the baptized ones were now walking in the sense of a new life as given by the Holy Spirit, and that by this act of baptism they were now being enrolled in that company which was to constitute "the church, which is his body." The mode by which this baptism was performed seems hardly to have been conscious to them. The first Christians were Jews; they thought of the Church as the remnant, the spiritual Israel, and they were accustomed to the various forms of baptism which had been common with their fathers. Sprinkling was representative of cleansing, the washing of the Holy Spirit, and was set forth in the great prophets, who represented the spiritual emphasis which Jesus came to make. The "baptism of John" signified a renewal of faith and religious activity in relation to the "coming kingdom." From the accounts given concerning his baptism surely it must have been by immersion. Earnest people in the days of Jesus were accustomed to the three modes, sprinkling, pouring, and immersion, just as Christians today observe them in the several churches, recognizing each as useful, legitimate baptism. There is no indication that during the first century the followers of Jesus considered the presence of these different modes in any way inconsistent or exclusive. "The physical act was not a question of conscience, hardly a question of consciousness. It did not belong in any vital sense to Christianity." There were simply these historic ways of symbolizing the inner, spiritual reality of religion, and of admission into the church. Only some centuries later, when the Church moved out from its Jewish inheritance of the emphasis upon the spiritual reality in religion, and its teachings came to be interpreted through the Gentile consciousness of the Roman world, did the strict, legal conception arise that salvation comes through the physical ceremony and therefore must be recieved always by a given form, immersion.

Bishop John M. Moore presents our Methodist view:

Why do Christians get from the New Testament different opinions of the mode of Baptism? Because the record of the conditions and circumstances under which the Baptism was administered creates and supports different opinions. The record is that John the Baptist baptized in the river Jordan, and that Jesus, upon being baptized "went up straightway out of the water." (Matt. 3:16.) That would suggest that John baptized by immersion, but it does not say so. Paul was stricken with blindness on his way to Damascus. Ananias visited him in his house, told him that Jesus had sent him, "that thou mightest receive thy sight, and be filled with the Holy Ghost." Paul "received sight forthwith, and arose and was baptized." (Acts 9: 17-18.) Evidently Ananias baptized him, and unless there was a pool in the house immersion was not practicable. The implication of the record is that Paul was baptized by sprinkling or by pouring water upon his head. But the record does not say so.

Philip preached Jesus to the eunuch of Ethiopia. They came to water. "They went down both into the water, both Philip and the eunuch; and he baptized him." (Acts 8:29-39.) That record would indicate that Philip immersed the eunuch, but it does not say so. The Philippian jailer was converted at midnight. "And he [Paul] took them the same hour of the night, and washed their stripes; and was baptized, he and all his, straightway." Unless there was a pool in the jail the baptism could hardly have been by immersion. The baptism of Cornelius and his household by Peter or those with him at Joppa (Acts 10:48), of Lydia and her family (Acts 16:15), of Stephanas and his family, were under circumstances and conditions which seem to make immersion impracticable and to make sprinkling or pouring desirable and reasonable. The New Testament records cited do not give conclusive proof for or against immersion, for or against sprinkling or pouring.[2]

[2] From *Methodism in Belief and Action*, copyright 1946 by Stone & Pierce. Used by permission of Abingdon-Cokesbury Press.

Jesus commanded that men be *baptized;* nowhere in the New Testament is he quoted as saying anything about the *mode* of that baptism. The New Testament certainly cannot be interpreted as giving clear evidence that any one mode was exclusive in its use, but indications are that sprinkling, pouring, and immersion were all used. There were the different ideas bound up in baptism—cleansing, commitment, initiation—and as the one or the other was being emphasized—during the New Testament times—the different modes were employed. Paul's account of "burial" represents a specific element in the common experience of conversion; but that element had been present in all ages, whenever men truly repented of their sins; so that that which Paul was describing was not new in Christian experience. He simply seized upon that illustration—as illustration—to emphasize this distinctly *inner* experience which he so greatly desired that his brethren should possess. There is absolutely no evidence in his passage to indicate that he was saying, If you are to be a Christian, you must be baptized in this way. He was saying, If you are to be a Christian, you must leave off your sins and take up a new way of life. And he used this mode of immersion in baptism to say it is like that. That same *new life* had been presented in the terms of the *cleansing* of the Holy Spirit and was represented by the application of water in sprinkling and pouring. But the use of sprinkling and pouring did not mean that this identical experience might not be represented by immersion.

John Wesley summed up in a paragraph what still seems to Methodists a fair statement concerning the mode of baptism:

142

Baptism is performed by washing, dipping, or sprinkling the persons, in the name of the Father, Son, and Holy Ghost. . . . I say, by washing, dipping, or sprinkling; because it is not determined in Scripture in which of these ways it shall be done, neither by any express precept, nor by any such example as clearly proves it; nor by the force or meaning of the word baptize.

Speaking before the American Bible Society in 1836, Stephen Olin said:

I thank God, sir, that we have no essential peculiarities. What we hold to be vital and most precious in religion, we hold in common with our brethren of other names. We hold nothing, we want nothing which ought to shut them out from our charities, nor, we verily believe, which should exclude us from theirs. Do they prefer an episcopal organization and government? Everybody knows we have no objection to that. Do they rejoice in presbytery? We claim no higher office or dignity. Are they congregational? We would that all God's people were prophets. Do they use forms of prayer? We often do the same. Do they extemporize their devotions? Our common practice shows that we think this a no less excellent way. Do they use much or little water in baptism? So the Spirit preside over the Sacrament—so the blessed auspices of Father, Son, and Holy Ghost be reconciled, it is all one to us whether the baptismal font be the ocean or a goblet. . . . Sir, I am a sincere Methodist, and might be found ready, if there were occasion for it, to vindicate the doctrines or usages of my Church; but I repeat it, I know of nothing in either incompatible with the largest charity and the most cordial cooperation with all who truly love the common Saviour.[3]

[3] William P. Strickland, *History of the American Bible Society*, pp. 447-48.

8.

Ordination in the Christian Church

THE CALL to preach rests upon the idea that the work of the ministry is essential to the salvation of souls. Paul states it as he writes to the Romans:

Brethren, my heart's desire and prayer to God for Israel is, that they might be saved. . . . The word is nigh thee, even in thy mouth . . . that if thou shalt confess with thy mouth the Lord Jesus, and shalt believe in thine heart that God hath raised him from the dead, thou shalt be saved. For with the heart man believeth unto righteousness; and with the mouth confession is made unto salvation. . . . For whosoever shall call upon the name of the Lord shall be saved. How then shall they call on him in whom they have not believed? and how shall they believe in him of whom they have not heard? and how shall they hear without a preacher?

If the spread of the gospel waits upon the preaching of the Word, then older ministers should help younger ones to hear and heed that call.

And Jesus went about all the cities and villages, teaching in their synagogues, and preaching the gospel of the kingdom, and healing every sickness and every disease among the people. But when he saw the multitudes, he was moved with compassion on them, because they fainted, and were scattered abroad, as sheep having no shepherd. Then saith he unto his disciples, The harvest truly is plenteous, but the labourers are few; pray ye therefore the Lord of the harvest, that he will send forth labourers into his harvest.

144

Like Paul and Timothy, every older preacher or layman may encourage younger ones in carrying out the work to which they have been called.

Thou therefore, my son, be strong in the grace that is in Christ Jesus. And the things that thou hast heard of me among many witnesses, the same commit thou to faithful men, who shall be able to teach others also. . . . I charge thee therefore before God, and the Lord Jesus Christ, who shall judge the quick and the dead. . . . Preach the word; be instant in season, out of season. . . . Watch thou in all things, endure afflictions, do the work of an evangelist, make full proof of thy ministry.

Jesus acknowledged his call:

And he came to Nazareth . . . and, as his custom was, he went into the synagogue. . . . And there was delivered unto him the book of the prophet Esaias. And when he had opened the book, he found the place where it was written, The Spirit of the Lord is upon me, because he hath anointed me to preach the gospel to the poor; he hath sent me to heal the brokenhearted, to preach deliverance to the captives, and recovering of sight to the blind, to set at liberty them that are bruised, to preach the acceptable year of the Lord. And he began to say unto them, This day is this scripture fulfilled in your ears.

Through all ages men have thought of God as calling persons into his service, laymen as well as ministers. Lord Ashley, a member of Parliament, was always busy in his work for the poor. When engaged in building a refuge for "thieves and ragged children," he is quoted as having said to his fellows: "Surely God has called me to this career." To William Wilberforce, author of the bill which was in the English House of Commons for forty years and which finally abolished slavery, Mr. Wesley wrote: "Go on, in the name of the Lord, until this sum of all villainies has been swept from the earth." It is the same understanding voiced

145

in the New Testament: "Paul an apostle—not from men nor through man, but through Jesus Christ and God the Father."

The ministry is initiated by the call; it is perpetuated by response through the character developed in the preacher.

> O for a heart to praise my God,
>   A heart from sin set free,
> A heart that always feels Thy blood
>   So freely shed for me!

And one cried unto another, and said, Holy, holy, holy, is the Lord of hosts: the whole earth is full of his glory. . . . Then said I, Woe is me! for I am undone; because I am a man of unclean lips, and I dwell in the midst of a people of unclean lips: for mine eyes have seen the King, the Lord of hosts. Then flew one of the seraphims unto me, having a live coal in his hand, which he had taken with the tongs from off the altar: and he laid it upon my mouth, and said, Lo, this hath touched thy lips; and thine iniquity is taken away, and thy sin purged. Also I heard the voice of the Lord, saying, Whom shall I send, and who will go for us? Then said I, Here am I; send me.

In the charge delivered as Francis Asbury was being ordained a bishop, Thomas Coke said:

Keep that which is committed to thy trust. Be not ashamed of the testimony of thy Lord, but a partaker of the afflictions of the Gospel according to the power of God. Endure hardships as a good soldier of Jesus Christ. Do the work of an evangelist, and make full proof of thy ministry; and thy God will open to thee a wide door, which all thy enemies shall not be able to shut. He will carry his gospel by thee from sea to sea, and from one continent to another.[1]

[1] Abel Stevens, *History of the Methodist Episcopal Church in the United States of America*, II, 185.

146

And then in the prayer, as he laid his hands of ordination on the head of Asbury, Coke continued:

> O Thou who art the Holy One and the True, consecrate this thy servant with the fire of divine love; separate him for thy glorious purpose; make him a star in thine own right hand; and fulfill in him, and by him, the good pleasure of thy goodness.[2]

Apart from the soul's individual welfare it has been Methodism's teaching that the seeking of holiness is that ministers may serve others. And so from our beginning days preachers have pleaded with the Almighty:

> That I thy mercy may proclaim,
> That all mankind thy truth may see,
> Hallow thy great and glorious name,
> And make holiness perfect in me.

And when the needs of the world become most urgent, then ministers grow more conscious of their unfitness; and they implore:

> Give me a new, a perfect heart,
> From doubt, and fear, and sorrow free;
> That mind which was in Christ impart,
> And let my spirit cleave to Thee.

HISTORIC CUSTOM OF ORDINATION

The laying on of hands, which was observed in New Testament times as well as in present-day ordination, was a familiar Jewish custom employed in the setting of men apart for a specific task or office. "As they ministered to the Lord, and fasted, the Holy Ghost said, Separate me Barnabas and Saul for the work whereunto I have called

[2] *Ibid.*

147

them. And when they had fasted and prayed, and laid their hands on them, they sent them away."

In another place the Scriptures record that when the people had selected their representatives and brought them to the apostles for formal installation, they prayed and "laid their hands on them." No explanation of the act is given, presumably because it was a matter of course to Jewish thinking; and no special virtue is attributed to it. It is simply a matter of order, a solemn delegation of office to men already marked out by spiritual endowments, recognized as such by the brethren among whom they have labored.

Throughout the Old Testament such an outward sign was used in setting apart for office, and so it is but to be expected that the same would be employed in the Christian Church. When he appointed Joshua as his successor Moses laid his hands on this man whom the Scriptures describe as already filled with the Spirit. Imposition of hands was used in dedicating sacrifices and in setting apart Levites for their work. Similarly Jesus blessed by laying on of hands and used the same symbolic act in healing. Apparently the service was not thought of either as magical or as conferring spiritual power; all the later, Catholic ideas about ordination as conferring *character*, enabling the minister to exercise the supernatural power to absolve men from their sins, seem entirely foreign either to Old Testament or to New Testament thought.

CATHOLIC CONCEPTION OF ORDINATION

When Christian congregations became sufficiently distinct from Jewish bodies to demand an organization and a ministry of their own, this familiar Old Testament form of installation was used. It was not applied to such as were called prophets, apostles, and teachers, seeing that Jesus had sent these men forth; this early ordination was at the hands of persons other than the Master, and this ceremony was had for those who had been selected by the congregation of believers, and so carried no authority other than that held by the group.

In later generations—beyond the days of the New Testament—when membership in the church came to be thought of as essential to salvation, ordination in like degree took on the quality of supernatural power. Thus the decrees of the Council of Trent, in the days of the Protestant Reformation, but officially assert what had been the teaching of the Catholic Church since the time of Cyprian and the third century: "If anyone saith that by sacred ordination the Holy Ghost is not given; and that vainly therefore do the bishops say, Receive ye the Holy Ghost; or that a character is not imprinted by that ordination; or that he who has once been a priest can again become a layman: let him be anathema."

PROTESTANT CONCEPTION OF ORDINATION

The Protestant conception of ordination is essentially different from that of Catholics because the Protestant understanding of God and man and the conditions of salvation is different from that held by Catholics. Protestantism goes back to the New Testament teaching that "by grace are ye saved *through* faith," whereas in practical usage the Catholic teaching is that "by grace are ye saved" *through the sacraments*. Not for one minute would a Protestant say that the Catholic Church does not require *faith* in the communicants as a ground of salvation, but it is only fair to

149

point out that the relation of faith to sacraments in the salvation process as maintained by Catholics is so greatly varied from the Protestant appreciation of faith as to warrant the distinction here made.

In Catholic doctrine, however earnest a man may be, he is simply unable to approach God directly. He may not make effective confession of sin to the Divinity alone; he must make that confession to the priest; and then the priest serves as mediator between man and God, to bring from God to man the absolution of sins. If man is really in that helpless condition, then surely his salvation depends upon the priest; and if the priest is to render so important a service to men, the priest needs to be infallibly and supernaturally qualified for his task.

But it is in this understanding of man's relation to God that Protestants do not see eye to eye with Catholics. Protestants read in the New Testament that Peter on the day of Pentecost called out to his brethren, "Repent ye, and be baptized every one of you in the name of Jesus Christ unto the remission of your sins; and ye shall receive the gift of the Holy Spirit." We do not find instruction there saying that the repentance should be made to the priest, and by the priest forwarded on to God, and forgiveness brought back to men by the priest.

In opposition to the Lutheran emphasis upon justification by faith the Council of Trent spoke the official teaching for all Catholics: "If any one saith that by the said sacraments of the New Law grace is not conferred through the act performed, but that faith alone in the divine promises suffices for the obtaining of grace: let him be anathema."

Against this conception that ministers capable of carrying on the work of the Church are "men to whom God by his appointed instruments has appointed certain authority and powers, a message of grace to be delivered and gifts of grace to be dispensed," Protestants cite the great commission of Jesus: "Go ye into all the world, and preach the gospel to every creature. He that believeth and is baptized shall be saved; but he that believeth not shall be damned."

Paul made much of the place of the preacher in salvation. Writing to his Roman friends, he shows his concern: "How then shall they call on him in whom they have not believed? and how shall they believe in him of whom they have not heard? and how shall they hear without a preacher?" But how different from the decrees of the Council of Trent is his emphasis upon individual confession and faith: "For with the heart man believeth unto righteousness; and with the mouth confession is made unto salvation. . . . For whosoever shall call upon the name of the Lord shall be saved."

If the Catholic interpretation of "grace" and "faith" is true, then surely for every man's salvation there must be a priest by ordination *infallibly qualified* to interpret sound doctrine, to receive confession, and to deliver forgiveness to repentant souls. Protestants do not so hold that estimate either of man's ability or of the value of ordination in the Christian ministry.

WHAT METHODISTS MEAN BY ORDINATION

Methodists have followed very closely the Protestant understanding and so look upon ministers as those who may instruct and guide seeking souls, but who of their own power are helpless to save even one sinful man. Growing out of its very genius—the doctrine that men are saved by faith in and obedience to God's will, and not through any ceremony or sanction exercised by a priest—such has been the teaching of our church. When one holds that conception of the church, and of the preachers as its agents, ordination can mean no more than an earnest setting of a man to the work of the ministry, just as it seems to have been employed in the first century of the Christian Church. Dr. John A. Kern, for many years professor of practical theology at Vanderbilt University, gave it as his matured conviction:

> The officers of a church do not differ, as to the possession of spiritual powers, from the people. No form of ordination makes any difference in this respect. When, for example, ordained ministers teach or preach or administer sacraments or preside in a business meeting or pronounce a benediction, we have no reason to believe that any spiritual influence attends their ministrations that might not attend the like ministrations at the hands of unordained ministers—as in the apostolic churches.[3]

In entire accord with this interpretation is the opinion of Bishop Thomas B. Neely:

> In other words, ordination is not so much in descent as in consent. It is not in the descent of any miraculous influence through the touch of the hands, but rather in the consent of the proper authority of the church, that the individual may administer a sacrament, as well as preach the gospel of our Lord Jesus Christ.[4]

GOD CALLS MEN TO BE MINISTERS

Probably no other teaching of the Church finds more widespread acceptance than that which declares that men are divinely called to be ministers. Catholic and Protestant

[3] John A. Kern, *Christianity as Organized*, p. 149.
[4] Thomas B. Neely, *Evolution of Episcopacy and Organic Methodism*, p. 205.

152

are one here; Methodists, Baptists, Presbyterians, Disciples of Christ, all insist upon its presence, and all hold that it must appear in so clear a manner that the would-be preacher realize it! But the *ceremony* in which this divine call is recognized is in no genuinely Protestant church looked upon as sharing in this supernatural character. Even more clearly the assignment to tasks and the division of preachers into grades, made by the church, claims nothing of the divine sanction. Personal fitness is the basis of such determination. If it feels that a man should go to the circuit, the church sends him there, without ordination for that specific type of service; and so to the station, or to the district superintendency, or to the college presidency, or to the secretaryship of a board. Bishop Warren A. Candler expressed this understanding of Methodism as follows:

God has signified in His Word that it is His will that certain men, whom He calls, shall devote themselves to the service of His Church; and that the Church shall recognize as its ministers persons giving evidence of such a divine call; shall appoint them to the ministry, authorize them to discharge the functions of the ministerial office. But as to the mode of their election, the forms and ceremonies of their ordination, the persons or officers by whom they shall be ordained, the division of their labors, and the ranks, classes, and orders into which they themselves shall be divided, the New Testament gives no distinct directions, and, therefore, as to these things there are no divine requirements; but the Church is left to determine them at its discretion.[5]

WHAT IS DONE FOR THE PREACHER IN ORDINATION?

For the half century of Methodism following its organization and the adoption of the constitution under which

[5] From the *Methodist Quarterly Review*, LXXI, 194. Copyright 1922 by Smith & Lamar. Used by permission of The Methodist Publishing House.

with few changes it operates today, probably no one has spoken in more intimate acquaintance with its ideals than has Dr. Nathan Bangs. Its earliest effective historian, a member of the General Conference, chosen by that body as editor of its official publications, Dr. Bangs earned a right to be heard as a leader of his denomination. For a number of years there raged among the churches in America a heated controversy over these very questions: the function of the church, the meaning of ordination, the validity of Methodist orders. First in a small volume, and twenty years later in an extended series of editorials, Dr. Bangs set forth his understanding of the Methodist position. In answer to the specific question: "What does ordination (or consecration) do for the candidate?" he wrote:

Consecration, it appears to me, is so far from imparting the qualifications of a minister, that it necessarily *presupposes* these qualifications, in the subject on whom the ceremony is performed. It strikes me most forcibly, that whatever may be the theory of some men on this subject, the *practice* of all denominations, with respect to the method adopted in receiving ministers at the altar, is founded on the presumption that certain qualifications are essential *before* consecration, to make a man a true minister of Jesus Christ.

What is the *practice* to which allusion is made? Do they not all *examine* the candidate in respect to his call, his qualifications, &c.? Of what is this examination predicated? Is it not that the candidate must possess certain qualifications, and even be "moved by the Holy Ghost to take upon him that office, "*before* he can be admitted to holy orders? Most certainly all this is implied. Nay, this inward call by the Holy Ghost, and certain mental and spiritual qualifications, are considered as *essential* prerequisites—so *essential* that if the person presenting himself as a candidate for the Christian ministry be judged destitute of them, his application is rejected.

What, then, it must be asked, does consecration do for the

154

person thus called and qualified? Does it impart any new gift? The words of consecration used in setting apart an elder, are as follows:—"The Lord pour upon thee the Holy Ghost for the office and work of an elder in the church of God, now committed unto thee by the imposition of our hands." That which is professed to be *committed* unto the person thus consecrated, is the *office and work of an elder in the church of God*, to which he had, as was believed by all concerned in this solemn transaction, been already called, and for which he is supposed to be fully qualified; and the prayer is, that the *Lord may pour upon him the Holy Ghost*, to fit him more perfectly for and to sustain him in his holy work. Here, therefore, is no new gift imparted, except so far as he is, by this public recognition of his character and official sanction of his professed call to the work of an elder in the church of God, authorized to exercise his gifts in that branch of the church of Christ.

The grand question therefore still remains to be answered,— *What does the act of consecration do for the man on whom it is performed?*

The only answer which seems any way satisfactory is, *that the act of consecration imparts authority to the incumbent to exercise those gifts which it is taken for granted he already possesses, in that particular branch of the church of Christ in which he thinks himself called to labor as a gospel minister.*[6]

ORDINATION ADDS SOMETHING NOT INCLUDED IN THE CALL
TO PREACH

Often it is asked: If the preacher has already received from the Holy Spirit the ability to speak as a minister in the name of the Lord, what is the function of ordination? And if the Almighty has really qualified men to labor in his kingdom, what right has a church to pass judgment upon a candidate's call and fitness for the work? Dr. Bangs reasoned on the assumption that there is a difference between (1) the call to preach and (2) the authority to speak

[6] Nathan Bangs, *An Original Church of Christ*, pp. 245-48.

155

as representative of a particular denomination. And underneath this relation of a denomination to any specific individual who might present himself, claiming to have been called to preach and asking to be a minister in that branch of the Church, Dr. Bangs explains that from the New Testament experience to the present every religious group has assumed that the Holy Spirit works through the Church, the body of older ministers, just as certainly as the Holy Spirit brings impression upon the mind of a particular individual. Therefore the Church as well as the individual has responsibility, to follow the direction of the Spirit; and churches have fulfilled this responsibility to persons offering themselves to become ministers, by examining the "candidate with respect to his call, his qualifications, etc."

A young man came to Wesley in the very early days of the Methodist movement, asking the privilege of "helping him in the gospel." At that time Wesley was hesitant, having held all his life the understanding of the Church of England, in which he was a minister, that only ordained men are able to "preach the gospel." But when his mother challenged him: "Take care what you do concerning this man, hear him for yourself, and see the fruits of his labors, for he is as surely called of God to preach as you are," Wesley listened to the young man and was convinced that "it is of the Lord." Thereupon Wesley said to him, "I will allow you to preach among the Methodists if you will agree to follow my directions."

All the churches, in all the ages, have required of candidates for the ministry such an "examination" as Wesley applied in "hearing" that young man and, as our church requires of preachers today in coming into "full connection." "Will you reverently heed them to whom the charge over you is committed?" Since 1746 the Methodist conference has made this test of a man's call to preach: "Does he have grace, does he have gifts, does he have fruits?" If favorable answer may be given to these questions, the young preacher may be admitted on trial in the ministry of The Methodist Church. In this way the older ministers meet their obligation to the Holy Spirit just as the younger minister does in responding to the call.

Concerning this authority to speak in the name of The Methodist Church, Dr. Bangs explained:

A man may be qualified to labor in any department of usefulness, as a mechanic, as a lawyer, or as a physician; but this does not entitle him to employ himself in any particular place, until he is authorized so to do by those to whom the place belongs, or over which they have control. So a man thinks himself called of God to preach the gospel. He examines the various modifications of Christianity as held and exemplified by the several denominations of Christians, and their methods of propagating them. Having made up his mind in regard to the truth and expediency of these, he presents himself to the denomination with which he thinks he can the most cordially unite. Here the proper officers of the church examine him in respect to his faith, experience of divine things, his knowledge and other qualifications; and if he give satisfactory evidence of his attainments in these things, he is accepted and consecrated; and by this solemn act he receives an authority he had not before to exercise his gifts to the edification of the church. . . . By this procedure "the gift" is imparted to him "with the laying on of hands of the presbytery," by which he is authorized to exercise himself as an accredited minister of Jesus Christ in that particular branch of the church, so long as he conforms to its ministerial requisitions, and no longer.[7]

What the church does in this relation, society at large

[7] *Ibid.*, p. 249.

carries out in its many public needs. The state assumes responsibility for providing proper educational facilities for all its children. However long any given man may have attended college, and whatever number of degrees he may have earned, no school board allows him to teach the children of its community until he has met the specific requirements found by experience to be proper in such a case. The economic welfare of the whole people demands such scrutiny of all men who would serve society in the capacity of attorneys, so formal bar examinations are held at given times each year in every state. It is not assumed that the bar examination will add to the prospective candidate any knowledge of the law which he did not possess before he stood that test, nor will the granting of a license to practice law bestow upon the young public servant any ability or quality of legal character not available to persons who have never applied for a "permit." Yet so concerned is society for the welfare of individuals whose property or life may be represented by the attorney that this official sanction is required of every man who would speak in the name of the law. Exactly such a requirement—and a very specific and revealing one—is prescribed for doctors and physicians. Like certification is becoming common in our day for all accountants who would make out income tax returns for their fellows, and for all agents who labor for the public good! It is simply that society is greater than any of its members, so has responsibility for the fortune and prosperity of the individual; and a community or state which today is remiss in such service to its citizens is held up to scorn.

Ordination is in the church as the teacher's certificate in public-school teaching, the license to practice law for the attorney, the state's permission given to men to prescribe

158

medicines for the health of its people. And as religion is of greater value to the individual than is education or law or medicine, then ordination stands in importance above the license of any other profession. Every denomination requires it, and they all find precedent in the Old Testament and in the New for such a "sending forth" of ministers into the work of the Church, in the form of prayer and the laying on of hands.

Methodism is at one with all our churches in the requirement of ordination of all ministers who would labor permanently in the work of the gospel, speaking in the name of The Methodist Church. At the same time Methodism has from its beginning kept clear in its teaching the difference between that which is done for the minister by the Holy Spirit, in the call to preach, and that which is signified by the laying on of hands in the ordination service. Again Nathan Bangs expressed the mind of today: "Does the ceremony of ordination make a man a minister of Jesus Christ, who is destitute of those other prerequisites? Is consecration in any branch of the church of Christ any thing more than a recognition that the individual consecrated has been 'called by the Holy Ghost to take upon him that office'?" [8] This view places Methodism in exact harmony with her sister denominations. On the nature of ordination the Cambridge Platform (for Congregationalists) declares: "Ordination we count nothing else but the solemn putting of a man into his place and office in the Church, whereunto he had right before by election." In similar vein is the statement of Dr. Hiscox for the Baptists: "Ordination does this for a man—this and nothing more—it accredits him to the churches and the public by the moral force which the approval and

[8] *Ibid.*, pp. 129-30.

commendation of the men engaged in the ordination service carries with it." So far as the conferring of "character" or "gifts" is concerned, the Presbyterian view accords with those given above: "Ordination is the solemn expression of the judgment of the Church, by those appointed to deliver such judgment, that the candidate is truly called of God to take part in this ministry, thereby authenticating to the people the divine call."

VALUE OF ORDINATION IN THE LIFE AND WORK OF THE PREACHER

Methodists believe that there is great value in the ordination ceremony. By it men who have felt themselves called of God to the work of the ministry are publicly and impressively set apart for that work. The religious denomination under whose supervision they propose to carry on their labors thus acknowledges them as its representatives and clothes them with whatever authority it may possess.

In his consciousness, as in that of the Church, he is thus placed in the ministry as a divine vocation, not as a mere profession. His ministry is the better for both his own sense of its sacredness and the impression of its sacredness in the mind of the Church. While there is no magical grace in the religious imposition of hands, there is a moral benefit. The man may still be living who has had a lifelong blessing in the remembered fact that when a boy Bishop Asbury laid his hand upon his head and invoked upon him the blessing of God. The imposition of the hand was not necessary to the invocation; yet it was from the same religious impulse, and a moral benefit went with it. There is such a manner of blessing in ordination. The seemly and impressive service is for good in the ordination of deacons, elders, and bishops.[9]

[9] John Miley, *Proceedings, Methodist Centennial Conference*, p. 117.